WI GUYS

Brilliant Thoughts and Big Talk from Real Men

Compiled by Allan Zullo

SOURCEBOOKS HYSTERIA™
AN IMPRINT OF SOURCEBOOKS, INC.®
NAPERVILLE, ILLINOIS

Published by Sourcebooks, Inc.
P.O. Box 4410, Naperville, Illinois 60567-4410
(630) 961-3900
FAX: (630) 961-2168
www.sourcebooks.com

ISBN 1-4022-0566-X

Printed and bound in Canada
WC 10 9 8 7 6 5 4 3 2 1

To my godson David Wartowski, an eager teacher and an even more eager learner.

—A.Z.

Maybe we are from Mars and don't stop for directions and covet the TV remote. Okay, so our needs aren't much greater than good sex, good food, and a good job—in that order. So what if getting emotional means getting teary-eyed over a fully restored '56 Chevy or bellowing in anguish over a dropped touchdown pass or ogling at the Hooters girls. None of that means we men aren't capable of expressing ourselves. In fact, *Wise Guys* proves that we aren't as clueless, witless, and mindless as the men who are portrayed in commercials and slammed in women's magazines.

In the following pages, you'll get some straight talk, big talk, and trash talk from great men and not-so-great men—from Socrates to Homer (Simpson, that is), from The Donald to the Don (Corleone), from Jimmy Buffett to Warren Buffett.

I hope these quotes will inspire, educate, or entertain you. Maybe they'll even trigger a lofty or clever notion of your own. But, hey, even if your original thoughts fall far short of the brilliant opinions, crackling observations, and shrewd perceptions collected in *Wise Guys*, feel free to steal any in this book for your own use. After all, the next best thing to being witty and wise is to quote from someone who actually is. As French Renaissance writer Michel de Montaigne once said, "I quote others only the better to express myself."

—A.Z.

When you die and go to heaven, our maker is not going to ask, "Why didn't you discover the cure for such and such?" "Why didn't you become the Messiah?" The only question we will be asked in that precious moment is "Why didn't you become you?"

—*Author, professor, and humanitarian Elie Wiesel*

In this world it is possible to achieve great material wealth, to live an opulent life. But a life built upon those things alone leaves a shallow legacy. In the end, we will be judged by other standards.

—*Labor activist and United Farm Workers Association founder Cesar Chavez*

Action

Action is a great restorer and builder of confidence. Inaction is not only the result, but the cause, of fear. Perhaps the action you take will be successful; perhaps different action or adjustments will have to follow. But any action is better than no action at all.

—Positive thinker and clergyman Dr. Norman Vincent Peale

I don't want planning. I want plans.

—General Electric CEO Jack Welch on what he expected from his middle managers

If you believe in what you are doing, then let nothing hold you up in your work. Much of the best work of the world has been done against seeming impossibilities. The thing is to get the work done.

—*Author and motivator Dale Carnegie*

Adventure

Nobody climbs mountains for scientific reasons. Science is used to raise money for the expeditions, but you really climb mountains for the hell of it.

—*Famed explorer Sir Edmund Hillary*

A large volume of adventures may be grasped within this little span of life by him who interests his heart in everything.

—Irish novelist Laurence Sterne

Adversity

When things are bad, we take comfort in the thought that they could always be worse. And when they are, we find hope in the thought that things are so bad that they have to get better.

—Publisher and adventurer Malcolm Forbes

The harder the conflict, the more glorious the triumph. What we obtain too cheap, we esteem too lightly; it is dearness only that gives everything its value. I love the man who can smile in trouble, who can gather strength from distress and grow brave by reflection. It is the business of little minds to shrink; but he whose heart is firm, and whose conscience approves his conduct, will pursue his principles unto death.

—*American revolutionary writer Thomas Paine*

All the adversity I've had in my life, all my troubles and obstacles, have strengthened me....You may not realize it when it happens, but a kick in the teeth may be the best thing in the world for you.

—*Disney empire founder, animator, and "imagineer" Walt Disney*

A word to the wise ain't necessary. It's the stupid ones who need the advice.

—Comedian Bill Cosby

It is better to give than receive... especially advice.

—Famed author and humorist Mark Twain

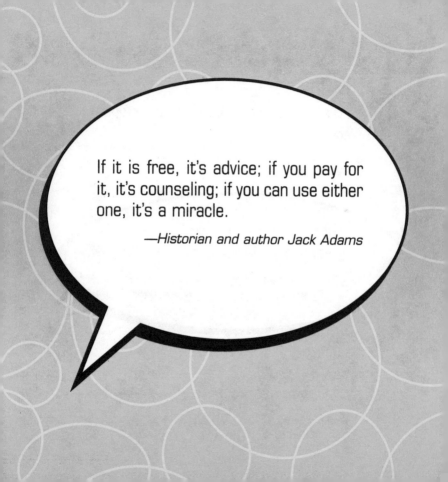

Don't do drugs, don't have unprotected sex, don't be violent.
Leave that to me.

—Rapper Eminem

Dream as if you'll live forever. Live as if you'll
die today.

*—Actor James Dean, who died in a
car crash at age 24*

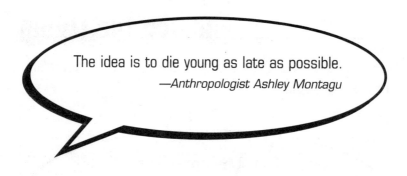

The idea is to die young as late as possible.
—*Anthropologist Ashley Montagu*

Avoid fried meats which angry up the blood. If your stomach disputes you, lie down and pacify it with cool thoughts. Keep the juices flowing by jangling around gently as you move. Go very light on the vices, such as carrying on in society. The social ramble ain't restful. Avoid running at all times. Don't look back. Something might be gaining on you.

—*Legendary pitcher Satchel Paige*

It's very simple. As you grow, you learn more. If you stayed at twenty-two, you'd always be as ignorant as you were at twenty-two. Aging is not just decay, you know. It's growth. It's more than the negative that you're going to die, it's also the positive that you understand you're going to die, and that you live a better life because of it.

—Brandeis University Professor of Sociology Morrie Schwartz, from the book Tuesdays with Morrie: An Old Man, A Young Man, and Life's Great Lesson *by Mitch Albom*

If I'd known I was gonna live this long, I'd have taken better care of myself.

—Musician Waylon Jennings

But no matter what your opinion may be of doctors, you'd better get used to dealing with them because as the warranty on your body starts to run out, you'll be spending more time in the shop than an E-Type Jag.

—*Comedian and talk-show host Dennis Miller*

Age is a high price to pay for maturity.

—*Czech-born playwright and author Tom Stoppard*

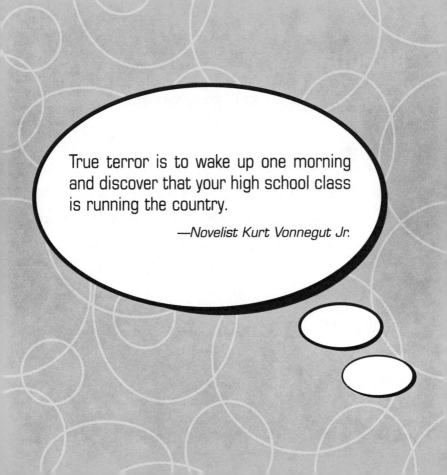

Altruism

It's easy to make a buck. It's a lot tougher to make a difference.

—Broadcaster Tom Brokaw

Any time you have an opportunity to make a difference in this world and you don't, then you are wasting your time on Earth.

—Pittsburgh Pirates Hall of Famer Roberto Clemente
shortly before he died in a plane crash while
delivering supplies to victims of a Nicaraguan earthquake

Whoever renders service to many puts himself in line for greatness—great wealth, great return, great satisfaction, great reputation, and great joy.

—*Motivational speaker and business coach Jim Rohn*

The best way to find yourself is to lose yourself in the service of others.

—*Political leader and icon of civil disobedience Mahatma Gandhi*

Ambition is a dream with a V8 engine.

—King of rock 'n' roll Elvis Presley

I'd rather be the shortest player in the majors than the tallest player in the minors.

—5-foot, 5-inch Kansas City Royals shortstop Freddie Patek

Ours is the only country deliberately founded on a good idea.

—*Journalist John Gunther*

In America, anybody can be president.
That's one of the risks you take.

—*Two-time Democratic presidential
candidate Adlai Stevenson*

Ain't nowhere else in the world but the good ol' USA where you can go from driving a truck to driving a Cadillac overnight. Nowhere.

—*King of rock 'n' roll Elvis Presley*

Ancestors

Remember, remember always, that all of us...are descended from immigrants and revolutionists.

—*32nd United States President Franklin Delano Roosevelt*

Anger

Temper's the one thing you can't get rid of by losing it.

—*Dr. Buddy Rydell (portrayed by Jack Nicholson),*
in the film Anger Management

Appearance

The uglier a man's legs are, the better he plays golf. It's almost a law.

—*Author H. G. Wells*

Great men are seldom over-scrupulous in the arrangement of their attire.
—*English novelist Charles Dickens*

Art

Creativity is allowing yourself to make mistakes. Art is knowing which ones to keep.

—Dilbert *comic strip creator Scott Adams*

All civilization and culture are the results of the creative imagination or artist quality in man. The artist...makes life more interesting or beautiful, more understandable or mysterious...more wonderful.

—Activist and artist George Bellows

The essence of all art is to have pleasure in giving pleasure.

*—Ballet dancer and actor
Mikhail Baryshnikov*

Atheism

I once wanted to become an atheist, but I gave up. They have no holidays.

—*Comedian Henny Youngman*

I'm just going to keep going and going and going until I can't go anymore.

—Allied Signals chairman Larry Bossidy

Things turn out best for the people who make the best out of the way things turn out.

—Radio and TV personality Art Linkletter

The greatest discovery of my generation is that human beings can alter their lives by altering their attitudes.

—Philosopher and psychologist William James

Authors

What I like in a good author is not what he says, but what he whispers.

—English-born writer Logan Pearsall Smith

Avocation

A hobby is only fun if you don't have the time to do it.

—Dutch-born soccer coach Leo Beenhakker

Babies

A baby is God's opinion that the world should go on.

—Poet Carl Sandburg

Bail-Out Plan

The first time I made a lot of money, I made them cut two checks. I gave one to the accountants, and I spent the other on a boat. When I started this whole thing, I thought that if I could make just enough money to buy a boat and find a bar to play in, I would be happy. And I still believe that. You have to have a bail-out plan all the time.

—Singer and songwriter Jimmy Buffett

Balance

Imagine life as a game in which you are juggling five balls in the air. You name them—work, family, health, friends, and spirit—and you're keeping all of these in the air. You will soon understand that work is a rubber ball. If you drop it, it will bounce back. But the other four balls—family, health, friends, and spirit—are made of glass. If you drop one of these, they will be irrevocably scuffed, marked, nicked, damaged, or even shattered. They will never be the same. You must understand that and strive for balance in your life.

—*CEO of Coca-Cola Enterprises Brian Dyson*

Baseball

Baseball's unique possession, the real source of our strength, is the fan's memory of the times his daddy took him to the game to see the great players of his youth.

—Baseball team owner and innovator Bill Veeck

Dottie Hinson (portrayed by Geena Davis), star player of a women's pro baseball team who wants to quit: "It just got too hard."

Manager Jimmy Dugan (portrayed by Tom Hanks): "It's supposed to be hard. If it wasn't hard, everyone would do it. The hard is what makes it great."

—From the film A League of Their Own

Thomas Jefferson never played baseball. If he had, he would have written that some men are more equal than others.

—High-school-teacher-turned-major-league-pitcher Jim Morris Jr., whose story was turned into the film The Rookie

Like life, basketball is messy and unpredictable. It has its way with you, no matter how hard you try to control it. The trick is to experience each moment with a clear mind and open heart. When you do that, the game—and life—will take care of itself.

—NBA coaching great Phil Jackson

Basketball forced me to deal head-on with my inadequacies and terrors with no room or tolerance for evasion. Though it was a long process, I learned to honor myself for what I accomplished in a sport where I was overmatched and out of my league. I never once approached greatness, but toward the end of my (college) career, I was always in the game.

—Author Pat Conroy, from his book My Losing Season

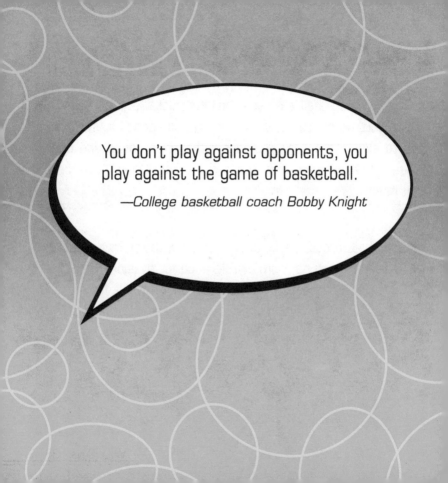

Being Good

Don't try to be different. Just be good. To be good is different enough.

—Singer, songwriter, and movie producer Arthur Freed

Belief

I have found that the greatest help in meeting any problem with decency and self-respect and whatever courage is demanded is to know where you yourself stand. That is, to have in words what you believe and are acting from.

—Novelist William Faulkner

Well, I believe in the soul…the small of a woman's back, the hangin' curveball, high fiber, good Scotch, that the novels of Susan Sontag are self-indulgent, overrated crap. I believe Lee Harvey Oswald acted alone, I believe there ought to be a constitutional amendment outlawing AstroTurf…I believe in the sweet spot, soft-core pornography, opening your presents Christmas morning rather than Christmas Eve, and I believe in long, slow, deep, wet kisses that last three days.

—*Crash Davis (portrayed by Kevin Costner),*
in the film Bull Durham

We cannot be sure of having something to live for unless we are willing to die for it.

—*Argentinean-born revolutionary Ernesto "Che" Guevara*

I would never die for my beliefs because I might be wrong.

—British philosopher and mathematician Bertrand Russell

Belief in Yourself

Somehow I can't believe that there are any heights that can't be scaled by a man who knows the secrets of making dreams come true. This special secret, it seems to me, can be summarized in four Cs. They are curiosity, confidence, courage, and constancy, and the greatest of all is confidence. When you believe in a thing, believe in it all the way, implicitly and unquestionably.

—Disney empire founder, animator, and "imagineer" Walt Disney

Anybody can do just about anything with himself that he really wants to and makes up his mind to do. We are capable of greater things than we realize.

—Positive thinker and clergyman Dr. Norman Vincent Peale

Whether you believe you can do a thing or not, you are right.

—Pioneering automaker Henry Ford

The Best

It's a funny thing about life; if you refuse to accept anything but the best, you very often get it.

—Novelist and playwright W. Somerset Maugham

Life is like a dogsled team. If you ain't the lead dog, the scenery never changes.

—Humorist Lewis Grizzard

Big Shots

The big shots are only the little shots who keep shooting.

—Journalist, poet, and novelist Christopher Morley

Blessings

Reflect upon your present blessings, of which every man has many; not on your past misfortunes, of which all men have some.

—English novelist Charles Dickens

Bliss

If you do follow your bliss, you put yourself on a kind of track that has been there all the while, waiting for you, and the life that you ought to be living is the one you are living. When you can see that, you begin to meet people who are in your field of bliss, and they open doors to you. I say, follow your bliss and don't be afraid, and doors will open where you didn't know they were going to be.

—Author and mythologist Joseph Campbell

Boldness

Live daringly, boldly, fearlessly. Taste the relish to be found in competition—in having put forth the best within you.

—*Industrialist Henry J. Kaiser*

Here's to alcohol: The cause of, and answer to, all of life's problems.

—Philosopher and American icon Homer Simpson

The three-martini lunch is the epitome of American efficiency. Where else can you get an earful, a bellyful, and a snootful at the same time?

—38th United States President Gerald R. Ford

Brains

It's what you learn after you know it all that counts.

—UCLA basketball coach John Wooden

Brainstorming

Thus, the task is, not so much to see what no one has yet seen; but to think what nobody has yet thought, about that which everybody sees.

—1933 Nobel Laureate in Physics Erwin Schrodinger

Bravery

Physical bravery is an animal instinct; moral bravery is a much higher and truer courage.

—*Antislavery crusader Wendell Phillips*

Bureaucracy

The only thing that saves us from bureaucracy is its inefficiency.

—*Former U.S. senator and 1968 Democratic presidential candidate Eugene McCarthy*

Businessmen

I find it rather easy to portray a businessman. Being bland, rather cruel, and incompetent comes naturally to me.

—English actor and comedian John Cleese

Business Strategy

Float like a butterfly and sting like a bee.

—Three-time world heavyweight champion Muhammad Ali

I don't want to kill everyone, Tom. Just my enemies.

—*Mafia boss Michael Corleone
(portrayed by Al Pacino),
in the film* The Godfather, Part II

Cats

Cats are intended to teach us that not everything in nature has a function.

—Prairie Home Companion *radio host and writer
Garrison Keillor*

I never want to get comfortable with what I'm doing. I don't think I can grow if I'm comfortable. So I want to push myself a little bit further.

—*Actor Nicholas Cage*

There is nothing like a challenge to bring out the best in man.

—*Scottish-born actor Sean Connery*

Change

I believe in change. It's the only thing I know of that's constant. When things stop changin', they die.

—*Country singer Conway Twitty*

Welcome change with open arms, but balance it while holding on to your basic values.

—*Spencer Johnson, MD, author of* Who Moved My Cheese?

They always say that time changes things, but you have to actually change them yourself.

—*Pop culture artist Andy Warhol*

I have no problem with change—I just don't want to be there when it happens.

—TV's obsessive-compulsive phobic detective Adrian Monk (portrayed by Tony Shalhoub)

If you want to make enemies, try to change something.

—28th United States President Woodrow Wilson

A person that is nice to you but rude to the waiter is not a nice person.

—Humorist and 1988 Pulitzer Prize winner Dave Barry

The real measure of our wealth is how much we'd be worth if we lost all our money.

—English Congregationalist J. H. Jowett

Our character is what we do when we think no one is looking.

—Author H. Jackson Brown Jr.

Charisma

Charisma: Some leaders have it, some leaders don't. The very best leaders have it in abundance. Deep down, every leader wants it. With a determined effort any leader can develop some degree of charisma. Like good leadership, charisma starts with an enthusiastic, positive, joyful approach to life in general. The inner strength, when properly cultivated and expressed, strikes a chord in others, enabling a leader to bring out the best in them. True caring about others is the critical element that translates the personality of a leader into the catalyst that results in charismatic leadership.

—U.S. Army Brigadier General John C. "Doc" Bahnsen,
who was awarded 18 medals for gallantry in Vietnam

Cheating

I'm a family person. I don't cheat on my wife. A man has to have principles. When you turn your back on your principles, you turn your back on yourself.

—*Country western star David Allan Coe*

Children

If kids are to be seen and not heard, why not just get some pictures of kids?

—*Political humorist Bill Maher*

Our greatest natural resource is the minds of our children.

—*Disney empire founder, animator, and "imagineer" Walt Disney*

Children have more need of models than of critics.

—French philosopher Joseph Joubert

Circumstantial Evidence

Circumstantial evidence can be very compelling. For instance, if, on a winter's night when you go to bed there is no snow on the ground and the next morning you awaken to two inches of the white stuff, it is all but certain that—though no one actually witnessed it—it snowed during the night.

—Prosecuter Thomas A. Wartowski

Civil Disobedience

An individual who breaks a law that conscience tells him is unjust, and who willingly accepts the penalty of imprisonment in order to arouse the conscience of the community over its injustice, is in reality expressing the highest respect for the law.

—*Civil rights icon Dr. Martin Luther King Jr.*

Close-mindedness

Hot heads and cold hearts never solved anything.

—Famed evangelist Billy Graham

Commercials

The Supreme Court says pornography is anything without artistic merit that causes sexual thoughts; that's their definition, essentially. No artistic merit, causes sexual thoughts. Hmm. Sounds like every commercial on television, doesn't it?

—Comedian Bill Hicks

Committees

My idea of a group decision is to look in the mirror.

—*Billionaire investor Warren Buffett*

Competition

It's all about ass. You either kick it or you lick it.

—*Arena football player Andy Jacobs*

In business, the competition will bite you if you keep running. If you stand still, they will swallow you.

—*Businessman Victor Kiam*

Competitive Spirit

If I were playing third base and my mother were rounding third with the run that was going to beat us, I'd trip her. Oh, I'd pick her up and brush her off and say, "Sorry, Mom," but nobody beats me.

—*Major League Baseball manager and player Leo Durocher*

Complaining

The man who complains about the way the ball bounces is likely the one who dropped it.

—College football coach Lou Holtz

Computers

Computers are useless. They can only give you answers.

—Artist Pablo Picasso

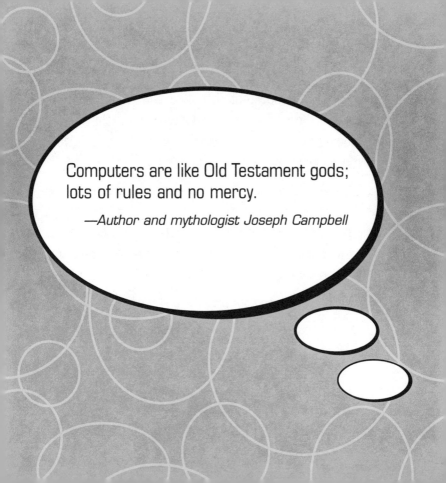

The function of RAM is to give us guys a way of deciding whose computer has the biggest, studliest, most tumescent MEMORY. This is important, because with today's complex software, the more memory a computer has, the faster it can produce error messages. So the bottom line is, if you're a guy, you cannot have enough RAM.

—*Humorist and 1988 Pulitzer Prize winner Dave Barry*

A computer lets you make more mistakes faster than any invention in human history—with the possible exception of handguns and tequila.

—*Internet content provider and analyst Mitch Ratcliffe*

In order to succeed, we must first believe that we can.

—Publisher Michael Korda

Don't let other people's lack of confidence in you stop you from trying. It's always great to prove them wrong.

—Country music star Travis Tritt

Confusion

I pretty much try to stay in a constant state of confusion just because of the expression it leaves on my face.

—*Actor Johnny Depp*

Conscience

When your intelligence don't tell you somethin' ain't right, your conscience gives you a tap on the shoulder and says, "Hold on." If it don't, you're a snake.

—King of rock 'n' roll Elvis Presley

Dig down deep in your heart and find out what's right, and that'll tell you what's wrong.

—Musician Waylon Jennings

Control

If everything seems under control, you're just not going fast enough.

—*Racecar driver Mario Andretti*

Country Music

You know what you get when you play country music backwards? You get your wife back, your house back, and your car back.

—*Country singer Clint Black*

Courage is what it takes to stand up and speak; courage is also what it takes to sit down and listen.

—*British prime minister Winston Churchill*

Courage is contagious. When a brave man takes a stand, the spines of others are stiffened.

—*Famed evangelist Billy Graham*

Courage is the greatest of all the virtues. Because if you haven't got courage, you may not have an opportunity to use any of the others.

—English writer Samuel Johnson

Courage is not simply one of the virtues, but the form of every virtue at the testing point.

—Irish-born writer C. S. Lewis

Crazy World

You know the world is going crazy when the best rapper is a white guy, the best golfer is a black guy, the tallest guy in the NBA is Chinese, the Swiss hold the America's Cup, France is accusing the U.S. of arrogance, Germany doesn't want to go to war, and the three most powerful men in America are named "Bush," "Dick," and "Colon."

—*Actor and comedian Chris Rock*

Creativity

A hunch is creativity trying to tell you something.

—*Film director Frank Capra*

What you really have to do, if you want to be creative, is to unlearn all the teasing and censoring that you've experienced throughout your life. If you are truly a creative person, you know that feeling insecure and lonely is par for the course. You can't have it both ways: You can't be creative and conform, too. You have to recognize that what makes you different also makes you creative.

—*1978 Nobel Laureate in Physics Arno Penzias*

Crisis

When written in Chinese, the word "crisis" is composed of two characters—one represents danger and the other represents opportunity.

—35th United States President John F. Kennedy

Criticism

If you are not criticized, you may not be doing much.

—U.S. Secretary of Defense Donald H. Rumsfeld

Customers

There is only one boss. The customer. And he can fire everybody in the company from the chairman on down, simply by spending his money somewhere else.

—*Wal-Mart founder Sam Walton*

Dark Side

People always have to guard themselves against their demons. Know what they are, and how to fight them. I've got that wild streak—that black dog inside of me that wants to bite—so I watch for signs that it's starting to growl.

—Music legend Johnny Cash

Daughters

The best gift you can give [daughters] is the truth about what those little 16- and 17-year-old boys are thinking....Just do what Charles Barkley said—kill the first [boy] and hope the word gets out.

—Actor and father of three daughters Bruce Willis

It is admirable for a man to take his son fishing, but there is a special place in heaven for the father who takes his daughter shopping.

—*Writer John Sinor,* author of
Some Ladies in My Life

Deadlines

I love deadlines. I like the whooshing sound they make as they fly by.

—*Author Douglas Adams,* creator of
The Hitchhiker's Guide to the Galaxy

Remember those posters that said, "Today is the first day of the rest of your life"? Well, that's true of every day but one—the day you die.

—*Lester Burnham (portrayed by Kevin Spacey),*
in the film American Beauty

After all, there are worse things in life than death. If you've ever spent an evening with an insurance salesman, you know what I'm talking about. The key is, to not think of death as an end, but as more of a very effective way to cut down on your expenses.

—*Boris Grushenko (portrayed by Woody Allen),*
in the film Love and Death

It is a blessing to die for a cause, because you can so easily die for nothing.

—African American leader, clergyman, and public official Andrew Young

Decision

In a world where death is the hunter, my friend, there is no time for regrets or doubts. There is only time for decisions.

—Metaphysical author Carlos Castaneda

Defeat

Defeat should never be a source of courage, but rather a fresh stimulant.

—*English clergyman Robert South*

I've learned something constructive from every defeat.

—*Dallas Cowboys coach Tom Landry*

Democracy is not something you believe in or a place to hang your hat, but it's something you do. You participate. If you stop doing it, democracy crumbles.

> —*Antiwar leader, social activist, author, and Chicago Seven defendant Abbie Hoffman*

Democracy does not guarantee equality of conditions—it only guarantees equality of opportunity.

> —*Neoconservative Irving Kristol*

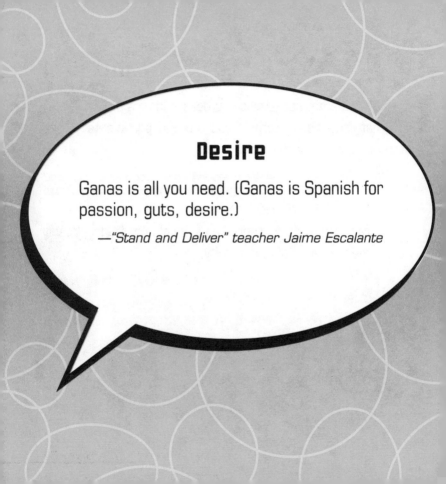

Desire

Ganas is all you need. (Ganas is Spanish for passion, guts, desire.)

—*"Stand and Deliver" teacher Jaime Escalante*

Destiny

It is time for martyrs now, and if I am to be one, it will be for the cause of brotherhood. That's the only thing that can save this country.

—American black nationalist and Muslim leader Malcolm X,
two days before his assassination

Details

Show me a big-picture guy and I'll show you a guy who's out of the picture.

—Costco CEO James Sinegal

Dignity

There's never sufficient reason to try to strip away another person's dignity.

—Speaker of the House Dennis Hastert, R-IL

Discouragement

Don't let life discourage you. Everyone who got where he is had to begin where he was.

—Radio minister Richard L. Evans

Discovery

One does not discover new lands without consenting to lose sight of the shore for a very long time.

—French critic and writer André Gide

Discretion

It's good to shut up sometimes.

—Internationally acclaimed mime Marcel Marceau

Diversity

Ultimately, America's answer to the intolerant man is diversity, the very diversity which our heritage of religious freedom has inspired.

—U.S. Senator and Attorney General Robert F. Kennedy

Do

Try not. Do, or do not. There is no try.

—Yoda, from the film The Empire Strikes Back

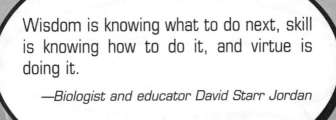

As I grow old, I pay less attention to what men say. I just watch what they do.

—*Industrialist and philanthropist Andrew Carnegie*

Saying is one thing and doing is another.

—*French essayist Michel de Montaigne*

Dogs

I love dogs. They live in the moment and don't care about anything except affection and food. They're loyal and happy. Humans are just too damn complicated.

—Actor David Duchovny of X-Files *fame*

Doing the Right Thing

The time is always right to do what is right.

—Civil rights icon Dr. Martin Luther King Jr.

Doing Your Best

It is not enough to do your best; you must know what to do, and then do your best.

—*Post-World War II government management consultant W. Edwards Deming*

It has never been my objective to record my dreams, just…to realize them.

—Artist Emmanuel "Man Ray" Radnitzky

It is better to risk starving to death then surrender. If you give up on your dreams, what's left?

—Comic actor Jim Carrey

All our dreams can come true, if we have the courage to pursue them.

—*Disney empire founder, animator, and "imagineer" Walt Disney*

Drinking

I was reading a periodical about wine the other day. And they had an ad for the "perfect breakfast wine." Let me tell you something. If you're drinking for breakfast, you don't care if it's perfect.

—The Tonight Show *host Jay Leno*

I distrust a man who says "when." If he's got to be careful not to drink too much, it's because he's not to be trusted when he does.

—Kasper Gutman (portrayed by Sydney Greenstreet), in the film The Maltese Falcon

Always do sober what you said you'd do drunk. That will teach you to keep your mouth shut.

—Famed author Ernest Hemingway

Earth

There are no passengers on Spaceship Earth. We are all crew.

—*Media and technology maven Marshall McLuhan*

Economics

Economics is simply common sense made difficult.

—*Economist Mark Vitner*

Education

In 100 years we have gone from teaching Latin and Greek in high school to teaching remedial English in college.

—*Columnist Joseph Sobran*

Sixty years ago I knew everything; now I know nothing; education is a progressive discovery of our own ignorance.

—*Philosopher and author Will Durant*

You cannot teach a man anything; you can only help him find it within himself.

—*Italian astronomer and mathematician Galileo Galilei*

The end of all education should surely be service to others.

—*Labor activist and United Farm Workers Association founder*
Cesar Chavez

Effort

I only know how to play two ways, and that's reckless and abandon.

—*NBA superstar Earvin "Magic" Johnson*

People say I don't have great tools. They say that I can't throw like Ellis Valentine or run like Tim Raines or hit with power like Mike Schmidt. Who can? I make up for it in other ways, by putting out a little bit more. That's my theory, to go through life hustling. In the big leagues, hustle usually means being in the right place at the right time. It means backing up a base. It means backing up your teammate. It means taking that head-first slide. It means doing everything you can do to win a baseball game.

—Baseball great Pete "Charlie Hustle" Rose

Ego

Ego is armor. People with the biggest egos, to a large degree, are probably the most insecure people you'll find. I know I am.

—Former Washington Redskins quarterback Joe Theismann

My dad used to say, "You wouldn't worry so much about what people thought of you if you knew how seldom they did."

—Psychologist and TV talk-show host Dr. Phil McGraw

Don't let your ego get too close to your position, so that if your position gets shot down, your ego doesn't go with it.

—Former Secretary of State Colin Powell

Emotions

You've got to be on the verge of tears and laughter every day. Those who keep their emotions inside, I feel sorry for. I cry easily and I laugh very easily. Opening ceremonies for the Olympics, I was crying my eyes out, holding hands with some plumber from Chicago.

—*North Carolina State basketball coach Jim Valvano*

Endeavor

You miss 100 percent of the shots you never take.

—*NHL Hall of Famer Wayne "The Great One" Gretzky*

Endurance

I learned from the example of my father that the manner in which one endures what must be endured is more important than the thing that must be endured.

—Former Secretary of State and presidential advisor Dean Acheson

Enemies

Forgive your enemies, but never forget their names.

—35th United States President John F. Kennedy

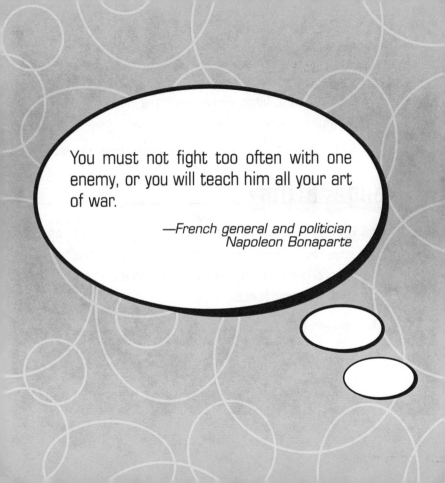

Entitlement

Don't believe the world owes you a living; the world owes you nothing. It was here first.

—*Humorist Robert Jones Burdette*

Exaggeration

The final key to the way I promote is bravado. I play to people's fantasies. People may not always think big themselves, but they can still get very excited by those who do. That's why a little hyperbole never hurts.

—*Businessman Donald Trump, from his book* The Art of the Deal

Executive Leadership

The best executive is the one who has sense enough to pick good men to do what he wants done, and self-restraint to keep from meddling with them while they do it.

—26th United States President Theodore Roosevelt

Expectations

The one thing I've always had going for me was people's low expectations. Nobody ever expects a whole hell of a lot from me.

—Musician and actor Chris Isaak

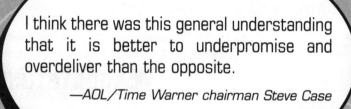

I think there was this general understanding that it is better to underpromise and overdeliver than the opposite.

—*AOL/Time Warner chairman Steve Case*

Experience

Part of my theory on getting to the top of a profession is that it's like mountain climbing. One way is you can climb your way to the top. The other way is that somebody can drop you off with a helicopter. The guy who climbed up there knows how to get back down, but the guy who got dropped off has to wait for another helicopter.

—*Singer and actor Kenny Rogers*

Explanation

Never explain. Your friends do not need it and your enemies will not believe you anyway.

—*Author and journalist Elbert Hubbard*

Extravagance

An extravagance is anything you buy that is of no earthly use to your wife.

—*Humorist Franklin P. Jones*

Facts

Facts are meaningless. You could use facts to prove anything that's even remotely true!

—*TV's iconic philosopher Homer Simpson*

I have not failed. I've just found 10,000 ways that won't work.

—Inventor Thomas Edison

I can accept failure. Everyone fails at something. But I can't accept not trying.

—Basketball great Michael Jordan

You know, to be able to do something great in your life, you're gonna have to realize your failures. You're gonna have to embrace them and figure out how to overcome it.

—*Comedian Dave Chappelle*

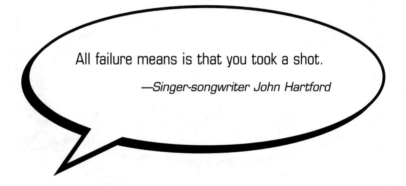

All failure means is that you took a shot.

—*Singer-songwriter John Hartford*

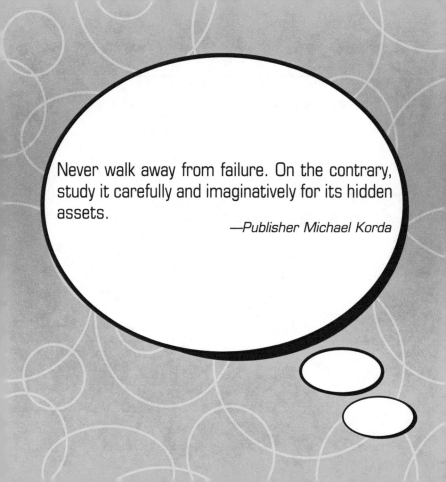

Faith

Faith is not belief without proof, but trust without reservation.

—*Quaker scholar D. Elton Trueblood*

I believe in the hereafter, and that this life is the training ground for it. That's why you better live like you're in the Lord's training camp, because you are.

—*Country star Merle Haggard*

The reason why birds can fly and we can't is simply that they have perfect faith, for to have faith is to have wings.

—Scottish playwright and novelist Sir James M. Barrie, author of Peter Pan

In faith there is enough light for those who want to believe and enough shadows to blind those who don't.

—French religious philosopher Blaise Pascal

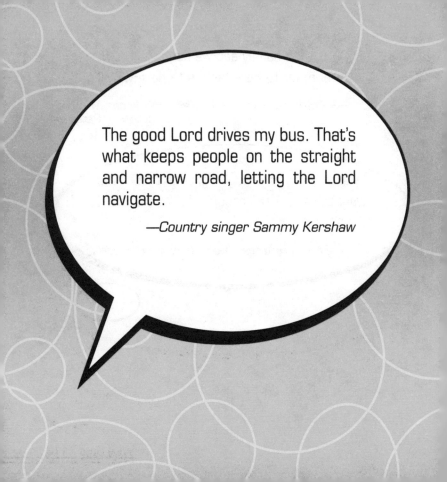

You know that point in your life when you realize the house you grew up in isn't really your home anymore? That idea of home is gone. Maybe that's all family really is. A group of people who miss the same imaginary place.

—*Andrew Largeman (portrayed by Zach Braff),*
in the film Garden State

As the family goes, so goes the nation and so goes the whole world in which we live.

—*Pope John Paul II*

Fast Food

I have a crucial rule for going to the drive-through. Never get behind a woman in a minivan. She's there to order food for the whole little league team.

—*Golfer Bobby Joe Grooves, from the novel* The Money-Whipped Steer-Job Three-Jack Give-Up Artist *by Dan Jenkins*

Fatherhood

To be a successful father there's one absolute rule: when you have a kid, don't look at it for two years.

—*Famed author Ernest Hemingway*

Any fool can make a baby, but it takes a real man to raise a child.

—*Jason "Furious" Styles (portrayed by Laurence Fishburne), in the film* Boyz 'N the Hood

It [fatherhood] gave me everything. A reason to live, a reason to learn, a reason to breathe, a reason to care.

—*Actor Johnny Depp*

What a father says to his children is not heard by the world, but it will be heard by posterity.

—*Seismologist Charles F. Richter*

Fatherhood is pretending the present you love the most is soap-on-a-rope.

—*Comedian Bill Cosby*

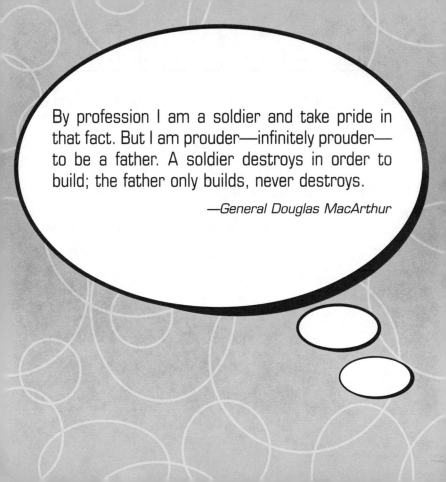

Fear

Show me a guy who's afraid to look bad, and I'll show you a guy you can beat every time.

—*St. Louis Cardinals base-stealer Lou Brock*

Fear defeats more people than any other one thing in the world.

—*Philosopher and poet Ralph Waldo Emerson*

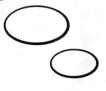

Fear is the most damnable, damaging thing to human personality in the whole world.

—*Novelist William Faulkner*

The thing we fear the most is not that we will shrivel up and become insignificant little people. The thing we fear the most is that we could become as big and grand as we are capable of becoming.

—*Former president of South Africa and
1993 Nobel Peace Prize winner Nelson Mandela*

Feeling

I don't sing a song unless I feel it. The song don't tug at my heart, I pass on it. I have to believe in what I'm doing.

—*Music legend Ray Charles*

Fickleness of Life

One day you can throw tomatoes through brick walls. The next day you can't dent a pane of glass with a rock.

—California Angels pitcher Dean Chance

Finding Answers

Perhaps we are not meant to know some things, for that is life too. A seeking. It may be our only purpose here.

—Actor Gabriel Byrne

Fine Details

When you catch your ass in a buzz saw, it's not too easy to tell how many teeth bit you.

—Official scorer to golf pro Brian Barnes, who asked for the score after 12-putting the eighth hole at the 1968 French Open

Fine Line

There's about a foot of difference between a halo and a noose.

—Florida State football coach Bobby Bowden

If fishing is a religion, then fly fishing is high church.

—*Broadcaster Tom Brokaw*

If I fished only to capture fish, my fishing trips would have ended long ago.

—*Author Zane Grey*

There is a fine line between fishing and just standing on the shore like an idiot.

—*Comedian Steven Wright*

Fleeting Fame

The whole world is drunk and we're just the cocktail of the moment. Someday soon, the world will wake up, down two aspirin with a glass of tomato juice, and wonder what the hell all the fuss was about.

—*Entertainer Dean Martin, at the height of his "Rat Pack" days*

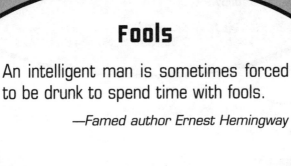

Who is more foolish? The fool, or the one who follows them?

—*Jedi Knight Ben Obi-Wan Kenobi (portrayed by Alec Guinness), in the film* Star Wars

Football

Football is a mistake. It combines the two worst elements of American life. Violence and committee meetings.

—*Political columnist George F. Will*

Let's face it, you have to have a slightly recessive gene that has a little something to do with the brain to go out on the football field and beat your head against other human beings on a daily basis.

—*Former NFL pro and TV game analyst Tim Green*

Pro football is like nuclear warfare. There are no winners, only survivors.

—*New York Giants Hall of Famer Frank Gifford*

Forgiveness

The weak can never forgive. Forgiveness is the attribute of the strong.

—Political leader and icon of civil disobedience Mahatma Gandhi

We must develop and maintain the capacity to forgive. He who is devoid of the power to forgive is devoid of the power to love. There is some good in the worst of us and some evil in the best of us. When we discover this, we are less prone to hate our enemies.

—Civil rights leader Dr. Martin Luther King Jr.

I had some bad old days. I always remember that God forgives, though, and one of the worst things you can do is not to forgive yourself.

—Music legend Johnny Cash

Fortitude

It is said an eastern monarch once charged his wise men to invent a sentence, to be ever in view, and which should be appropriate in all times and situations. They presented him with the words, "And this, too, shall pass away." How much it expresses! How chastening in the hour of pride! How consoling in the depths of affliction!

—*16th United States President Abraham Lincoln*

Frame of Mind

I have never been poor, only broke. Being poor is a frame of mind. Being broke is only a temporary situation.

—*Showman and film producer Mike Todd*

There is only one basic human right, the right to do as you damn well please. And with it comes the only basic human duty, the duty to take the consequences.

—*Writer and political satirist P. J. O'Rourke*

Freedom is nothing else but a chance to be better.

—*French existential writer and 1957 Nobel Laureate in Literature Albert Camus*

Aye, fight and you may die. Run, and you'll live. At least a while. And dying in your beds, many years from now, would you be willing to trade all the days from this day to that...for one chance...just one chance to come back here to tell our enemy that they may take out lives, but they will never take our freedom!

—*Scottish hero Sir William Wallace (portrayed by Mel Gibson),
in the film* Braveheart

We look forward to a world founded upon four essential human freedoms. The first is freedom of speech and expression—everywhere in the world. The second is freedom of every person to worship God in his own way...everywhere in the world. The third is freedom from want...everywhere in the world. The fourth is freedom from fear—anywhere in the world.

—*32nd United States President Franklin Delano Roosevelt,
in his 1941 State of the Union address*

Free Will

I do not feel obliged to believe that the same God who has endowed us with sense, reason, and intellect has intended us to forego their use.

—*Italian astronomer and mathematician Galileo Galilei*

It is possible to become discouraged about the injustice we see everywhere. But God did not promise us that the world would be humane and just. He gives us the gift of life and allows us to choose the way we will use our limited time on earth. It is an awesome opportunity.

—*Labor activist and United Farm Workers Association founder Cesar Chavez*

People pay for what they do, and still more for what they have allowed themselves to become. And they pay for it very simply; by the lives they lead.

—*Author James Baldwin*

The loss of a friend is like that of a limb; time may heal the anguish of the wound, but the loss cannot be repaired.

—*English writer Robert Southey*

My father always used to say that when you die, if you've got five real friends, then you've had a great life.

—*Businessman and industrialist Lee Iacocca*

Funerals

They say such nice things about people at their funerals that it makes me sad that I'm going to miss mine by just a few days.

—Prairie Home Companion *radio host and writer Garrison Keillor*

The Future

What I look forward to is continued immaturity followed by death.

—*Humorist and 1988 Pulitzer Prize winner Dave Barry*

I never think of the future. It comes soon enough.

—German-born American physicist Albert Einstein

Gambling

A dollar won is twice as sweet as a dollar earned.

—Pool player Fast Eddie Felson (portrayed by Paul Newman),
in the film The Color of Money

If I lose today, I can look forward to winning tomorrow, and if I win today, I can expect to lose tomorrow. A sure thing is no fun.

—*Comic actor Chico Marx*

The next best thing to gambling and winning is gambling and losing.

—*Oddsmaker Jimmy "The Greek" Snyder*

Gays

Why can't they have gay people in the army? Personally, I think they are just afraid of a thousand guys with M16s going, "Who'd you call a faggot?"

—*Comedian and talk-show host Jon Stewart*

Generosity

The value of a man resides in what he gives and not in what he is capable of receiving.

—*German-born American physicist Albert Einstein*

Geniuses

The fact that some geniuses were laughed at does not imply that all who are laughed at are geniuses. They laughed at Columbus, they laughed at Fulton, they laughed at the Wright brothers. But they also laughed at Bozo the Clown.

—*Astronomer Carl Sagan*

Girls

The trouble with girls is, if they like a boy, no matter how big a bastard he is, they'll say he has an inferiority complex, and if they don't like him, no matter how nice a guy he is, or how big an inferiority complex he has, they'll say he's conceited. Even smart girls do it.

—Holden Caulfield, from the novel The Catcher in the Rye *by J. D. Salinger*

Giving

We make a living by what we get, but we make a life by what we give.

—British prime minister Winston Churchill

Glory

Glory is not a conceit. It is not a decoration for valor. Glory belongs to the act of being constant to something greater than yourself, to a cause, to your principles, to the people on whom you rely and who rely on you in return.

—*Arizona Senator and former Vietnam POW John McCain*

Goals

The indispensable first step to getting the things you want out of life is this: decide what you want.

—*Actor and author Ben Stein*

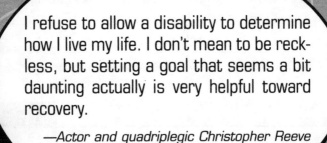

I refuse to allow a disability to determine how I live my life. I don't mean to be reckless, but setting a goal that seems a bit daunting actually is very helpful toward recovery.

—Actor and quadriplegic Christopher Reeve

A man has to know what he wants to do, and then do it and keep his mind on it, and don't let nothing else get in the way to clutter up his life.

—Country western legend Hank Williams

God

Let me give you a little inside information about God. God likes to watch. He's a prankster. Think about it. He gives man instincts. He gives you this extraordinary gift, and then what does He do? I swear for His own amusement, His own private, cosmic gag reel, He sets the rules in opposition. It's the goof of all time. Look, but don't touch. Touch, but don't taste. Taste, but don't swallow. Ahaha. And while you're jumpin' from one foot to the next, what is he doing? He's laughin' His sick, fuckin' ass off. He's a tight-ass. He's a sadist. He's an absentee landlord. Worship that? Never.

—John Milton, AKA the devil, (portrayed by Al Pacino),
in the film The Devil's Advocate

My deeply held belief is that if a god of anything like the traditional sort exists, our curiosity and intelligence is provided by such a god. We would be unappreciative of that gift...if we suppressed our passion to explore the universe ourselves.

—Astronomer Carl Sagan

God didn't make skyscrapers or pollution or crowded streets. The deity we all believe in made mountains, streams, horses and other animals, and a lot of fish. I figure he must be a cowboy.

—Country singer Dan Seals

If only God would give me some clear sign! Like making a large deposit in my name at a Swiss Bank.

—Film director Woody Allen

Everything else can wait, but the search for God cannot.

—Beatle George Harrison

If I were not an atheist, I would believe in a God who would choose to save people on the basis of the totality of their lives and not the pattern of their words. I think he would prefer an honest and righteous atheist to a TV preacher whose every word is God, God, God, and whose every deed is foul, foul, foul.

—Author Isaac Asimov

It is the final proof of God's omnipotence that he need not exist in order to save us.

—Short-story writer and novelist Peter de Vries

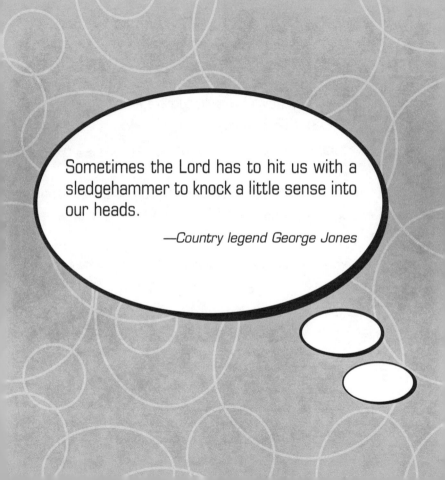

Golf

I like golf because you can be really terrible at it and still not look much dorkier than anybody else.

—Humorist and 1988 Pulitzer Prize winner Dave Barry

So, it's me again, huh, Lord? Why don't you just come down here and we'll play. And bring that kid of yours. I'll play your best ball.

—Temperamental golf pro Tommy Bolt, after blowing a putt

It took me 17 years to get 3,000 hits in baseball.
I did it in one afternoon on the golf course.

—Hall of Fame slugger Henry "Hank" Aaron

Good Loser

Show me a good loser and I'll show you a seldom winner.

—Golfing legend Sam Snead

Government

Can any of you seriously say the Bill of Rights could get through Congress today? It wouldn't even get out of committee.

—*Famed attorney F. Lee Bailey*

Giving money and power to government is like giving whiskey and car keys to teenage boys.

—*Author and political satirist P. J. O'Rourke*

The best minds are not in government. If they were, business would hire them away.

—*40th United States President Ronald Reagan*

A government big enough to give you everything you want is a government big enough to take from you everything you have.

—*38th United States President Gerald R. Ford*

Gratitude

Of all the attitudes we can acquire, surely the attitude of gratitude is the most important and by far the most life-changing.

—Super salesman and motivator Zig Ziglar

The world is so exquisite, with so much love and moral depth, that there is no reason to deceive ourselves with pretty stories for which there's little good evidence. Far better, it seems to me, in our vulnerability, is to look Death in the eye and to be grateful every day for the brief but magnificent opportunity that life provides.

—Astronomer Carl Sagan

Great Minds

Great minds discuss ideas, average minds discuss events, small minds discuss people.

—*U.S. Navy Admiral Hyman Rickover*

Greed

The point is, ladies and gentlemen, is that greed—for lack of a better word—is good. Greed is right. Greed works. Greed clarifies, cuts through, and captures the essence of the evolutionary spirit. Greed, in all of its forms—greed for life, for money, for love, knowledge—has marked the upward surge of mankind. And greed—you mark my words—will not only save Teldar Paper, but that other malfunctioning corporation called the U.S.A. Thank you very much.

—*Address by corporate raider Gordon Gekko*
(portrayed by Michael Douglas) to the stockholders of Teldar Paper,
in the film Wall Street

Growing Old

I always liked the number 80. But I think you pass a certain border at that point. There are not that many good writers at 80. My knees are old, my hearing is going, and some of my senses are diminished. But my brain is not too old, maybe 50. I have always looked upon aging as analogous to being an old freighter, and to sail through heavy seas you have to throw some things overboard. You give up certain senses. In my case, I wanted to keep my mind reasonably alive.

—*Novelist Norman Mailer*

If you live to be one hundred, you've got it made. Very few people die past that age.

—*Comedian and actor George Burns, who lived to see 100*

Guys

I have a hammer! I can put things together! I can knock things apart! I can alter my environment at will and make an incredible din all the while! Ah, it's great to be male!

—*Calvin, from the comic strip* Calvin and Hobbes *created by Bill Watterson*

Guys are simple…women are not simple and they always assume that men must be just as complicated as they are, only way more mysterious. The whole point is guys are not thinking much. They are just what they appear to be. Tragically.

—*Humorist and 1988 Pulitzer Prize winner Dave Barry*

Happiness

Happiness and success not only do not run around together; it is doubtful they even know one another.

—*Country western singer Tom T. Hall*

Look solely for happiness, and I doubt you'll find it. Forget about happiness, seek wisdom and goodness, and probably happiness will find you. Happiness is usually indirect, a side-effect or by-product of something else.

—*Psychiatrist M. Scott Peck, author of* The Road Less Traveled

Happiness is like a cat—if you coax it or call it, it will avoid you; it won't come. But if you pay no attention to it and go about your business, you will find it rubbing against your legs and jumping into your lap. So forget pursuing happiness. Instead, pursue learning, pursue work, pursue honor, pursue your commitments and keep them, pursue the truth, pursue decency, look honestly for God. Be faithful to your spouse, your children, to your friends, to your country.

—*Author and former Secretary of Education William J. Bennett*

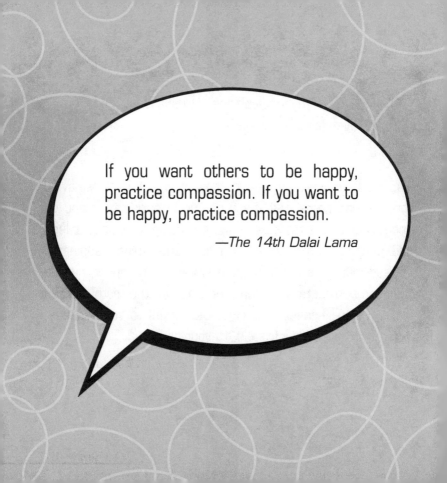

Always stop and remember that happiness doesn't come from having everything you want, but in understanding and accepting all, and in the prayer and belief that everything always happens for the best.

—Country western star Willie Nelson

Hard Work

Both tears and sweat are salty, but they render a different result. Tears will get you sympathy; sweat will get you change.

—Civil rights activist Jesse Jackson

Health

You've got to work at living—99 and 9/10ths of Americans work at dying. You've got to eat right, exercise, and have goals and challenges. Exercise is king; nutrition is queen. Put 'em together and you've got a kingdom.

—*Godfather of fitness Jack LaLanne at age 90*

Hell

The safest road to Hell is the gradual one—the gentle slope, soft underfoot, without sudden turnings, without milestones, without signposts.

—*Author C. S. Lewis*

Holidays

The proper behavior all through the holiday season is to be drunk. This drunkenness culminates on New Year's Eve, when you get so drunk you kiss the person you're married to.

—*Writer and political satirist P. J. O'Rourke*

Hope

Hope arouses, as nothing else can arouse, a passion for the possible.

—*Clergyman and activist William Sloane Coffin Jr.*

Remember, Red. Hope is a good thing, maybe the best of things and no good thing ever dies. I will be hoping that this letter finds you, and finds you well.

—*Excerpt of a letter from escaped prisoner Andy Dufresne (portrayed by Tim Robbins) to paroled prisoner Ellis Boyd "Red" Redding (portrayed by Morgan Freeman), in the film* The Shawshank Redemption

The Human Condition

After one look at this planet, a visitor from outer space would say, "I want to see the management."

—*Beat writer William S. Burroughs*

Human Nature

Nothing defines humans better than their willingness to do irrational things in the pursuit of phenomenally unlikely payoffs.

—*Cartoonist and author Scott Adams, from his book* The Dilbert Principle

Human Rights

America did not invent human rights. In a very real sense, it is the other way around. Human rights invented America.

—39th United States President Jimmy Carter,
who won the Nobel Peace Prize in 2002

Human Spirit

Difficulties are meant to rouse, not discourage. The human spirit is to grow strong by conflict.

—Author, antislavery activist, and Unitarian clergyman
William E. Channing

Imagination was given to man to compensate him for what he isn't. A sense of humor was provided to console him for what he is.

—*English novelist Horace Walpole*

Humor is just another defense against the universe.

—*Producer, writer, and comedian Mel Brooks*

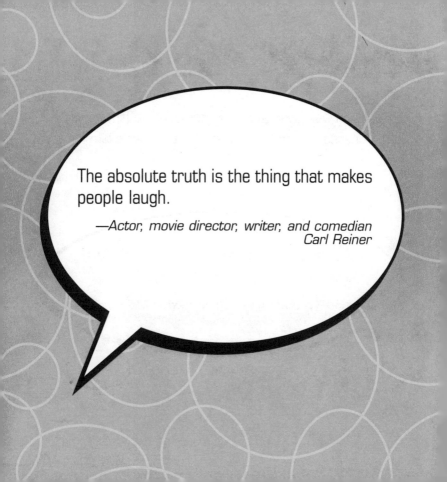

Hunting is not a sport. In a sport, both sides should know they're in the game.

—*Comedian Paul Rodriguez*

Society will forever judge hunters by their compassion for the animals they hunt.

—*Outdoor writer and radio talk-show host Jim Slinsky*

Idealism

Idealism is fine, but as it approaches reality the cost becomes prohibitive.

—*Conservative wit, columnist, and author William F. Buckley Jr.*

Ideal Woman

I'm gonna go out and find me a girl who can suck the chrome off a trailer hitch.

—*Country western star Willie Nelson*

Good ideas are not adopted automatically. They must be driven into practice with courageous patience.

—*U.S. Navy Admiral Hyman Rickover*

The creation of a thousand forests is in one acorn.

—*Philosopher and poet Ralph Waldo Emerson*

The need to be right all the time is the biggest bar to new ideas. It is better to have enough ideas for some of them to be wrong than to be always right by having no ideas at all.

—Educator, lecturer, and thinker Edward de Bono

There is one thing stronger than all the armies of the world, and that is an idea whose time has come.

—French author and poet Victor Hugo

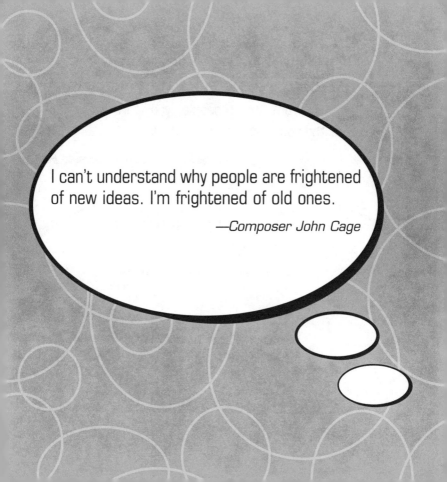

Idiots

You don't learn from smart people, you learn from idiots.
Watch what they do, and then don't do it.

—Famed pool hustler Minnesota Fats

There is nothing more dangerous than a
resourceful idiot.

—Working class icon Dilbert, *created by*
Scott Adams

If "ifs" were gifts, every day would be Christmas.

—NBA great Charles Barkley

A great deal of intelligence can be invested in ignorance when the need for illusion is deep.

—Author and 1976 Nobel Laureate in Literature Saul Bellow

Image

The more people know about you, the less they want to know. Don't ever lose your mystique.

—*Country singer Conway Twitty*

The only thing necessary for the triumph of evil is for good men to do nothing.

—*British politician Edmund Burke*

Even if you're on the right track, you'll get run over if you just sit there.

—*Humorist Will Rogers*

Indifference

The opposite of love is not hate, it's indifference. The opposite of art is not ugliness, it's indifference. The opposite of faith is not heresy, it's indifference. And the opposite of life is not death, it's indifference.

—Author, professor, and humanitarian Elie Wiesel

Inner Peace

We can never obtain peace in the world if we neglect the inner world and don't make peace with ourselves. World peace must develop out of inner peace.

—The 14th Dalai Lama

Innovation

Innovation doesn't come from the big company. It never has and never will. Innovation is something new that looks crazy at first glance. It comes from the 19-year-olds and the start-ups that no one's heard of.

—Cofounder of Internet pioneer Netscape Communications Corp.
Marc Andreessen

Innovation distinguishes between a leader and a follower.

—CEO of Apple Computers and Pixar Animation Studios
Steve Jobs

Integrity

With integrity you have nothing to fear, since you have nothing to hide. With integrity you will do the right thing, so you will have no guilt. With fear and guilt removed, you are free to be and do your best.

—*Super salesman and motivator Zig Ziglar*

Somebody once said that in looking for people to hire, you look for three qualities: integrity, intelligence, and energy. And if they don't have the first, the other two will kill you. You think about it; it's true. If you hire somebody without the first, you really want them to be dumb and lazy.

—*Billionaire investor Warren Buffett*

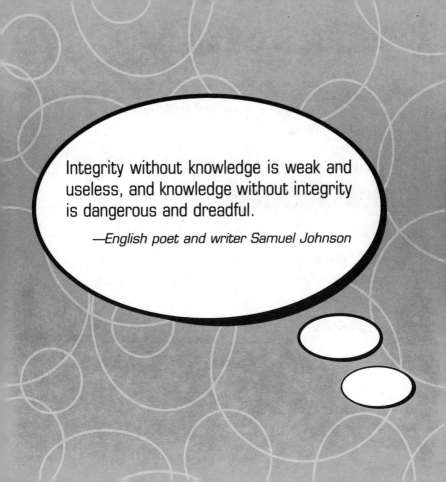

Intensity

If you make every game a life-and-death proposition, you're going to have problems. For one thing, you'll be dead a lot.

—North Carolina basketball coach Dean Smith

Introspection

Only barbarians are not curious about where they come from, how they came to be where they are, where they appear to be going, whether they wish to go there, and if so, why, and if not, why not.

—Latvian-born philosopher, historian, and essayist Isaiah Berlin

The battles that count aren't the ones for gold medals. The struggles within yourself—the invisible, inevitable battles inside all of us—that's where it's at.

—Olympic track and field gold medalist Jesse Owens

Jazz

Man, if you gotta ask, you'll never know.

—Trumpet player extraordinaire Louis "Satchmo" Armstrong,
when asked what jazz is

Jesus

He never asked anyone to become a Christian, never built a steepled building, never drew up a theological treatise, never took an offering, never wore religious garments, never incorporated for tax purposes. He simply called people to follow him.

—*Author Don Everts,*
from Jesus with Dirty Feet

As attorneys, we operate in a legal system where our stated purpose is to achieve justice for our clients. My clients, however, prefer victories over justice.

—*Attorney Danny Manausa*

Though justice moves slowly, it seldom fails to overtake the wicked.

—*Roman poet and satirist Horace*

I tell ye Hogan's right when he says, "Justice is blind." Blind she is, an' deef an' dumb an' has a wooden leg!

—*Mr. Dooley, a character created by American humorist Finley Peter Dunne*

You might not find justice in the courtroom, but you usually get what you deserve.

—*Attorney David Spicer*

Keeping Things in Perspective

If you break your neck, if you have nothing to eat, if your house is on fire, then you got a problem. Everything else is inconvenience.

—Theologian, philosopher, and author Robert Fulghum

Know It All

The only fool bigger than the person who knows it all is the person who argues with him.

—Polish writer Stanislaw Jerzy Lec

Knowledge

Knowledge comes, but wisdom lingers.

—English poet Alfred, Lord Tennyson

Real knowledge is to know the extent of one's ignorance.

—Chinese philosopher and teacher Confucius

Labor

Labor was the first price, the original purchase-money that was paid for all things. It was not by gold or by silver, but by labor that all wealth of the world was originally purchased.

—*Founder of modern economics Adam Smith*

Laughing at Yourself

Happy is the person who can laugh at himself. He will never cease to be amused.

—Former Tunisian president Habib Bourguiba

Laughter

Be thankful for laughter except when milk comes out of your nose.

—Comedian Steve Martin

Lawmen

When you're a lawman and you're dealin' with people, you do a whole lot better if you go not so much by the book, but by the heart.

—*Sheriff Andy Taylor (portrayed by Andy Griffith),*
from The Andy Griffith Show

Laws

Laws are spider webs; they hold the weak and delicate who are caught in their meshes, but are torn in pieces by the rich and powerful.

—*Scythian philosopher Anacharsis*

A lawyer with a briefcase can steal more than a hundred men with guns.

> —*Don Corleone, in the novel* The Godfather *by Mario Puzo*

Of course I have lawyers. They are like nuclear weapons. I've got 'em 'cuz everyone else has 'em. But as soon as you use 'em, they mess everything up.

> —*Corporate raider Lawrence Garfield (portrayed by Danny DeVito), in the film* Other People's Money

Some people think that a lawyer's business is to make white black; but his real business is to make white in spite of the stained and soiled condition which renders its true color questionable. He is simply an intellectual washing machine.

—*Judge Logan E. Bleckley*

Leadership

Leadership is unlocking people's potential to become better.

—*Former NBA star and New Jersey senator Bill Bradley*

Treat a person as he is, and he will remain as he is. Treat him as he could be, and he will become what he should be.

—*Former college and NFL football coach*
Jimmy Johnson

Learning

My biggest motivation? Just to keep challenging myself. I see life almost like one long university education that I never had—every day I'm learning something new.

—*British entrepreneur Richard Branson*

I have learnt silence from the talkative, tolerance from the intolerant, and kindness from the unkind.

—Lebanese-born writer Kahlil Gibran, author of The Prophet

The important thing is to learn a lesson every time you lose. Life is a learning process, and you have to try to learn what's best for you. Life is not fun when you're banging your head against the wall.

—Tennis player John McEnroe

Human beings, who are almost unique in having the ability to learn from the experience of others, are also remarkable for their apparent disinclination to do so.

—*Author Douglas Adams, creator of* The Hitchhiker's Guide to the Galaxy

Liberty

Let every nation know, whether it wishes us well or ill, that we shall pay any price, bear any burden, meet any hardship, support any friend, oppose any foe to assure the survival and the success of liberty.

—35th United States President John F. Kennedy

Life

Life moves pretty fast. If you don't stop and look around once in a while, you could miss it.

—Ferris Bueller (portrayed by Matthew Broderick),
in the film Ferris Bueller's Day Off

Hope for the best, expect the worst. Life is a play. We're unrehearsed.

—*Producer, writer, and comedian Mel Brooks*

Ordinary life is pretty complex stuff.

—*Comic book writer Harvey Pekar*
of American Splendor *fame*

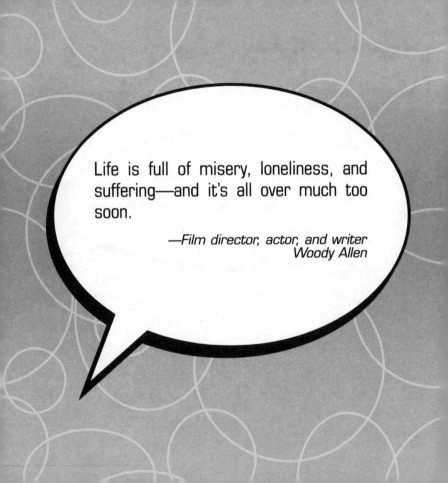

The examined life is no picnic.

*—Theologian, philosopher, and author Robert Fulghum, from his
book* All I Really Need to Know I Learned in Kindergarten

An unexamined life is not worth living.

—Greek philosopher Socrates

It's a shallow life that doesn't give a person a few scars.

—Prairie Home Companion *radio host and writer Garrison Keillor*

I'm not a fan of real life. Real life's got some strange kind of rules.

—*Actor Nick Nolte*

Every day you're still above ground is a good day.

—Mafia underboss Salvatore "Sammy the Bull" Gravano,
whose testimony led to the convictions of 36 mobsters

Life is like music; it must be composed by ear, feeling, and instinct, not by rule.

—English author Samuel Butler

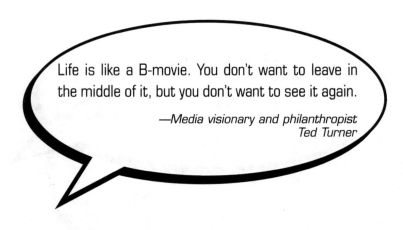

Life is like a B-movie. You don't want to leave in the middle of it, but you don't want to see it again.

—*Media visionary and philanthropist Ted Turner*

Life is intrinsically, well, boring and dangerous at the same time. At any given moment the floor may open up. Of course, it almost never does; that's what makes it so boring.

—*Author and illustrator Edward Gorey*

Life and Death

I'd rather die today and go to heaven than live to be a hundred and go to hell.

*—Preacher Euliss "Sonny" Dewey (portrayed by Robert Duvall),
in the film* The Apostle

We cannot truly face life until we face the fact that it will be taken away from us.

—Famed evangelist Billy Graham

Despite everybody who has been born and has died, the world has just gone on. I mean, look at Napoleon—but we went right on. Look at Harpo Marx—the world went around, it didn't stop for a second. It's sad but true.

—*Songwriter and performer Bob Dylan*

Life Lessons

The reason you have a bad experience is to teach you not to do it again.

—*Country western star Willie Nelson*

Listening

I've never learned anything while I was talking.

—*Talk-show host Larry King*

What a different world this would be if people would listen to those who know more and not merely try to get something from those who have more.

—*Presbyterian minister William J. H. Boetcker*

Literature

Literature is the memory of humanity.

—*Polish-born American novelist and 1978 Nobel Laureate in Literature Isaac Bashevis Singer*

Living Life

Death is not the greatest loss of life. The greatest loss is what dies inside us while we live.

> —*Editor and writer Norman Cousins, from his book*
> Anatomy of an Illness

You have to live Plan A—on any level. Make it a lowercase "a" if you have to, but live your Plan A. Anything else belittles the importance of life.

> —*Actor Vin Diesel*

Life is truly a ride. We're all strapped in and no one can stop it. When the doctor slaps your behind, he's ripping your ticket and away you go. As you make each passage from youth to adulthood to maturity, sometimes you put your arms up and scream, sometimes you just hang on to that bar in front of you. But the ride is the thing. I think the most you can hope for at the end of life is that your hair's messed, you're out of breath, and you didn't throw up.

—*Jerry Seinfeld, from his book* SeinLanguage

You'll have time to rest when you're dead.

—*Actor Robert De Niro*

Your life is not going to be easy, and it should not be easy. It ought to be hard. It ought to be radical; it ought to be restless; it ought to lead you to places you'd rather not go.

—*Dutch-born priest, psychologist, theologian, and activist Henri Nouwen*

This is a great truth, one of the greatest truths. It is a great truth because once we truly see this truth, we transcend it. Once we truly know that life is difficult—once we truly understand and accept it—then life is no longer difficult. Because once it is accepted, the fact that life is difficult no longer matters.

—*Psychiatrist M. Scott Peck, author of* The Road Less Traveled

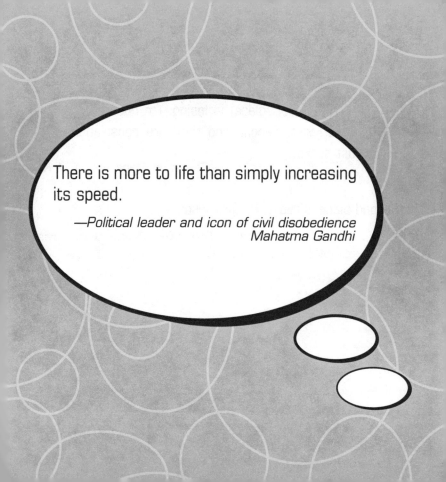

Losing

Anything below first [place] is losing. I'm not satisfied with anything but first. Second and third are consolations, and fourth just sucks.

—*Champion Alpine skier A. J. Kitt*

Second place is really the first loser.

—*New York Yankees owner George Steinbrenner*

A heart is not judged by how much you love, but by how much you are loved by others.

> —*The Wizard of Oz (portrayed by Frank Morgan),*
> *in the film* The Wizard of Oz

Passion makes the world go round. Love just makes it a safer place.

> —*Rapper and actor Ice-T*

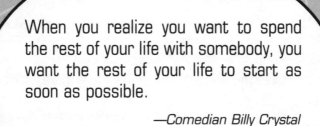

Peggy Bundy: "Tell me you love me, Al."
Al Bundy: "I love football, I love beer, let's not cheapen the meaning of the word."

—*From the TV show* Married With Children

There are only four questions of value in life, Don Octavio. What is sacred? Of what is the spirit made? What is worth living for, and what is worth dying for? The answer to each is the same: only love.

—*Don Juan (portrayed by Johnny Depp),
in the film* Don Juan De Marco

Lois Griffin: "Peter. You're bribing your daughter with a car?"
Peter Griffin: "Ah, c'mon, Lois, isn't 'bribe' just another word for 'love'?"

—*From the animated TV show* Family Guy

Luck

I believe in luck. How else can you explain the success of those you dislike?

—*French writer, poet, and artist Jean Cocteau*

If there is any realistic deterrent to marriage, it's the fact that you can't afford divorce.

—*Actor Jack Nicholson*

Nobody, man or woman, has ever wrecked a good marriage.

—*Singer, actor, and sausage maker Jimmy Dean*

Women marry men hoping they will change. Men marry women hoping they will not. So each is inevitably disappointed.

—German-born American physicist Albert Einstein, who divorced once and married twice

To me, the difference between being single and married is the form of government. When you're single, you are the dictator of your own life. You have complete power. When I give the order to fall asleep on the sofa with the TV on in the middle of the day, no one can overrule me! When you are married, you are part of a vast decision-making body. Before anything is accomplished, there's got to be meetings, committees have to study the situation.

—Comedian Jerry Seinfeld, from his book SeinLanguage

The value of marriage is not that adults produce children, but that children produce adults.

—Short-story writer and novelist Peter De Vries

Men

Fifty percent of America's population spends less than $10 a month on romance. You know what we call these people? Men.

—Tonight Show *host Jay Leno*

Mind

The only man who can change his mind is a man that's got one.

—Novelist Edward Westcott

Miracles

Believe in miracles but don't depend on them.

—Author H. Jackson Brown Jr.

Misperception

Once upon a time a man whose axe was missing suspected his neighbor's son. The boy walked like a thief, and spoke like a thief. But the man found his axe while digging in the valley, and the next time he saw his neighbor's son, the boy walked, looked, and spoke like any other child.

—*Chinese philosopher Lao Tzu, father of Taoism*

If you let every mistake you make trip you up, you'll be doing nothing but stumbling the rest of your life.

—Country western star David Allan Coe

A life spent making mistakes is not only more honorable, but more useful than a life spent doing nothing.

—Irish author, playwright, and socialist George Bernard Shaw

Mistakes are a part of being human. Appreciate your mistakes for what they are: precious life lessons that can only be learned the hard way. Unless it's a fatal mistake, which, at least, others can learn from.

—Political commentator and comedian Al Franken

Don't apologize for every failure. I've made about every mistake a man can make, and even repeated a few of 'em.

—Country music singer Johnny Paycheck

Money is a terrible master but a wonderful servant.

—Circus promoter P. T. Barnum

The safest way to double your money is to fold it over once and put it in your pocket.

—Humorist Frank McKinney "Kin" Hubbard

Money couldn't buy you friends, but you get a better class of enemy.

—British comedian Spike Milligan

Monogamy

For all you men that think having 1,000 different women is cool, I have found that having one woman 1,000 different times is really the way to go.

—Basketball great Wilt Chamberlain, who claimed to have slept with 20,000 women

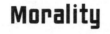

Morality

I'm a moral person, but I think, like most people, my moral values are pretty fuzzy.

—*Rolling Stone Mick Jagger*

The world has achieved brilliance without wisdom, power without conscience. Ours is a world of nuclear giants and ethical infants.

—*General Omar Bradley*

In the moral life, as in life itself, we take one step at a time.

—*Author and former U.S. Secretary of Education*
William J. Bennett

Mama was the one who reached down and tied my shoelace. Mama spit on her fingers and used it to clean dirt off my face.

—*Funnyman Adam Sandler*

I hope they're still making women like my momma. She always told me to do the right thing. She always told me to have pride in myself; she said a good name is better than money.

—*World heavyweight boxing champion Joe Louis*

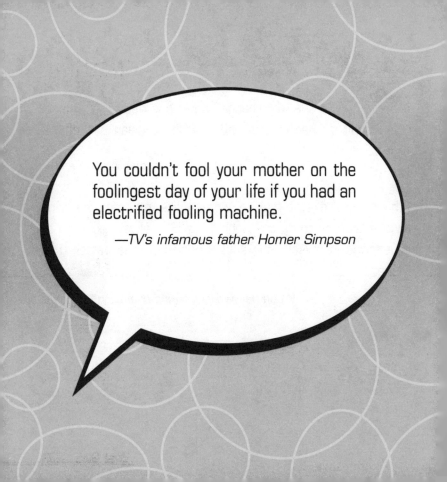

Mountain Climbing

Climbers, as a species, are simply not distinguished by an excess of prudence. And that holds especially true for Everest climbers: when presented with a chance to reach the planet's highest summit, history shows, people are surprisingly quick to abandon good judgment.

—Author and climber Jon Krakauer, from his book Into Thin Air

Music

You need music... We need magic and bliss, and power, myth, and celebration, and religion in our lives, and music is a good way to encapsulate a lot of it.

—Grateful Dead great Jerry Garcia

I think my music is like anchovies—some people love it, some people get nauseous.

—Singer and songwriter Barry Manilow

Music is the soundtrack of your life.

—Producer, director, host, and iconic disc jockey Dick Clark

I think of music as a menu. I can't eat the same thing everyday.

—*Mexican-born musician Carlos Santana*

Newspapers

They kill good trees to put out bad newspapers.

—*Ronald Reagan's Secretary of the Interior James G. Watt*

In revealing the workings of government that led to the Vietnam War, the newspapers nobly did precisely that which the Founders hoped and trusted they would do.

—*Supreme Court Justice Hugo L. Black*

Obituary

When my obituary notice at last appears in The Times, and they say: "What? I thought he died years ago," my ghost will gently chuckle.

—*English novelist and playwright William Somerset Maugham*

Obstacles

Obstacles are those frightful things you see when you take your eyes off your goal.

—*Pioneering automaker Henry Ford*

Obstacles don't have to stop you. If you run into a wall, don't turn around and give up. Figure out how to climb it, go through it, or work around it.

—*Chicago Bulls superstar Michael Jordan*

Conquering any difficulty always gives one a secret joy, for it means pushing back a boundary line and adding to one's liberty.

—*Swiss philosopher Henri Amiel*

Oil

As for geopolitical concerns that we shouldn't be dependent for our energy on people who hate us, that sword has two edges. The producing countries need oil revenues at least as much as we need oil. If they stop pumping, we would carpool, but they would starve.

—*Economist Stephen J. Entin*

Opportunity

Opportunity is missed by most people because it is dressed in overalls and looks like work.

—*Inventor Thomas Edison*

Optimism

Positive belief at the start of a doubtful undertaking is often the one thing ensuring its successful outcome.

—*Politician and orator William Jennings Bryan*

Outrage

I want you to get up right now and go to the window. Open it and stick your head out and yell, "I'm mad as hell, and I'm not going to take this anymore!"

—Anchorman Howard Beale (portrayed by Peter Finch),
in the film Network

Outspokenness

I do say things that I think will shock people. But I don't do things to shock people. I'm not trying to be the next Tupac, but I don't know how long I'm going to be on this planet. So while I'm here, I might as well make the most of it.

—Rapper Eminem

Pain

Pain is your friend, your ally. It will tell you when you are seriously injured. It will keep you awake and angry and remind you to finish the job and get the hell home. But you know the best thing about pain? It lets you know you're not dead yet.

—Master Chief John Urgayle (portrayed by Viggo Mortensen),
in the film GI Jane

Parenthood

Having a child is the most beautifully irrational act that two people in love can commit.

—Comedian Bill Cosby

Past, Present, and Future

Yesterday is a cancelled check. Today is cash on the line. Tomorrow is a promissory note.

—Kansas City Chiefs coach Hank Stram

Patriotism

Patriotism never goes out of style.

—Lee "God Bless the U.S.A." Greenwood

A patriot must always be ready to defend his country against his government.

—*Ecology author and iconoclast Edward Abbey*

Peace

The soldier, above all other people, prays for peace, for he must suffer and bear the deepest wounds and scars of war.

—*General Douglas MacArthur*

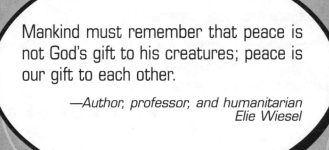

Perfection

A man can travel far and wide—all the way to shame or glory, and back again—but he ain't never gonna find nothin' in this old world that's dead solid perfect.

—Author Dan Jenkins, from his book Dead Solid Perfect

Have no fear of perfection—you'll never reach it.

—Spanish painter Salvador Dali

You only have to bat 1.000 in two things—flying and heart transplants. Everything else you can go four for five.

—ESPN SportsCenter analyst Beano Cooke

Nothing would be done at all if a man or woman waited until they could do it so well that no one could find fault with it.

—British cleric John Henry Cardinal Newman

Perseverance

My motto was always to keep swinging. Whether I was in a slump or feeling badly or having trouble off the field, the only thing to do was keep swinging.

—Hall of Fame slugger Henry "Hank" Aaron

Our greatest glory is not in never falling, but in rising every time we fall.

—Chinese philosopher Confucius

Persistence

Nothing in this world can take the place of persistence. Talent will not; nothing is more common than unsuccessful people with talent. Genius will not; unrewarded genius is almost a proverb. Education will not; the world is full of educated derelicts. Persistence and determination alone are omnipotent. The slogan "press on" has solved and always will solve the problems of the human race.

—*30th United States President Calvin Coolidge*

Ambition is the path to success. Persistence is the vehicle you arrive in.

—*Former NBA star and New Jersey senator Bill Bradley*

Personal Finance

Live beyond your means; then you're forced to work hard, and you have to succeed.

—*Actor Edward G. Robinson*

Personal Responsibility

You must take personal responsibility. You cannot change the circumstances, the seasons, or the wind, but you can change yourself. That is something you have charge of.

—*Motivational speaker and business coach Jim Rohn*

Perspective

Success isn't permanent and failure isn't fatal.

—Former Chicago Bears and New Orleans Saints coach
Mike Ditka

Well, here's my problem with pro sports today. I don't care whether it's football, basketball, or baseball. Guys are complaining about making $6 million instead of $7 million, and what is their job? Playing a damned game. You know what I made last year? I made $14,000. They pay me $14,000 and you know what my job description is? I'm paid to take a bullet.

—An anonymous Marine in San Diego (the site of
Super Bowl XXXVII) the night before shipping out across the
Pacific toward Iraq, from a January 22, 2003, column by
St. Louis Post-Dispatch *writer Bryan Burwell*

Pessimism

I have a lot of energy, and I can direct it either positively or negatively. I've found that when I direct it negatively, a lot of bad things happen—mostly to me.

—Country western star Willie Nelson

Philosophy

Live and let live, that's what I say. Anyone who can't under-stand that should be killed. It's a simple philosophy, but it's always worked well in our family.

—*Comedian George Carlin, from his book*
Napalm and Silly Putty

My philosophy has always been to shoot straight and make sure you're the one still standing. Then take your loved one's hand and move it on. More than that, no one can ask for. And more than that, no one really needs.

—*Country western star Willie Nelson*

Poetry

We don't read and write poetry because it's cute. We read and write poetry because we are members of the human race, and the human race is filled with passion.

—John Keating (portrayed by Robin Williams) to his students, in the film Dead Poets Society

Poker

If you're playing a poker game and you look around the table and can't tell who the sucker is, it's you.

—Actor Paul Newman

Politics

Politics is supposed to be the second-oldest profession. I have come to realize that it bears a very close resemblance to the first.

—*40th United States President
Ronald Reagan*

I have come to the conclusion that politics are too serious a matter to be left to the politicians.

—French general and president Charles de Gaulle

Possibilities

Become a "possibilitarian." No matter how dark things seem to be or actually are, raise your sights and see the possibilities—always see them, for they're always there.

—Positive thinker and clergyman Dr. Norman Vincent Peale

Poverty

Wars on nations change maps. War on poverty maps change.

—Three-time world heavyweight champion Muhammad Ali

Power

In this country, you gotta make the money first. Then when you get the money, you get the power. Then when you get the power, then you get the women.

—Tony Montana (portrayed by Al Pacino),
in the film Scarface

Donkey: "Hey, what's your problem, Shrek? What do you got against the whole world?"

Shrek: "Look, I'm not the one with the problem, OK? It's the world that seems to have a problem with me. People take one look at me and go, 'Ahhh...run...a big stupid ugly ogre!' They judge me before they even know me. That's why I'm better off alone."

—*Dialogue from the film* Shrek

Prejudice is a great time saver. You can form opinions without having to get the facts.

—*Author and essayist E. B. White*

Everyone is a prisoner of his own experiences. No one can eliminate prejudices—only recognize them.

—Famed broadcaster Edward R. Murrow

Principles

Above all, we must realize that no arsenal, or no weapon in the arsenals of the world, is so formidable as the will and moral courage of free men and women. It is a weapon our adversaries in today's world do not have.

—40th United States President Ronald Reagan

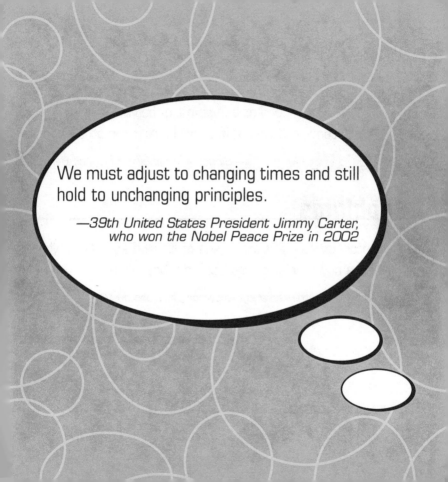

Priorities

Of the five most important things in life, health is first, education is second, and wealth is third. I forget the other two.

—*Singer and songwriter Chuck Berry*

Problems

Every problem has in it the seeds of its own solution. If you don't have any problems, you don't get any seeds.

—*Positive thinker and clergyman Dr. Norman Vincent Peale*

Don't tell people about your problems. Ninety percent of the people don't care and the other 10 percent are glad you've got them.

—*College football coach Lou Holtz*

If you can't solve the problem, manage it.

—*"Hour of Power" televangelist Rev. Robert Schuller*

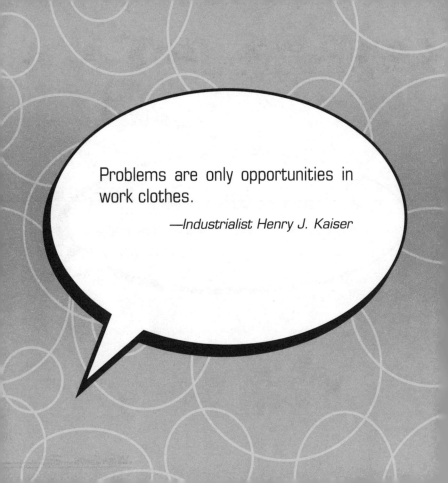

Procrastination

Procrastination is opportunity's assassin.

—Businessman Victor Kaim

Purpose

This is our purpose: to make as meaningful as possible this life that has been bestowed upon us...to live in such a way that we may be proud of ourselves, to act in such a way that some part of us lives on.

—German philosopher Oswald Spengler

Quotations

I pick my favorite quotations and store them in my mind as ready armor, offensive or defensive, amid the struggle of this turbulent existence.

—*Scottish poet Robert Burns*

A fine quotation is a diamond in the hand of a man of wit and a pebble in the hand of a fool.

—*French artist Joseph Roux*

Racial Unity

There can be no black-white unity until there is first some black unity.

—*American black nationalist and Muslim leader Malcolm X*

Racing

If you're not a race driver, stay the hell home. Don't come here and grumble about going too fast. Get the hell out of the racecar if you've got feathers on your legs and butt. Put a kerosene rag around your ankles so the ants won't climb up there and eat that candy ass.

—*NASCAR legend Dale Earnhardt, who died in a crash at the 2001 Daytona 500*

Racism

Racism isn't born, folks, it's taught. I have a two-year-old son. You know what he hates? Naps. End of list.

—Actor Denis Leary

Reading

The failure to read good books both enfeebles the vision and strengthens our most fatal tendency—the belief that the here and now is all there is.

—Author and educator Allan Bloom

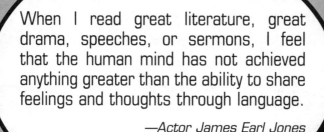

Realist

An idealist believes the short run doesn't count. A cynic believes the long run doesn't matter. A realist believes that what is done or left undone in the short run determines the long run.

—Strictly Personal *columnist Sydney J. Harris*

Reality

Reality is that which, when you stop believing in it, doesn't go away.

—*Science fiction writer Philip K. Dick*

I believe in looking reality straight in the eye and denying it.

—Prairie Home Companion *radio host and writer*
Garrison Keillor

Life is what happens while you're busy making other plans.

—*Beatle John Lennon*

Religion

Science without religion is lame, religion without science is blind.

—*German-born American physicist Albert Einstein*

Life in Lubbock, Texas, taught me two things: One is that God loves you and you're going to burn in hell. The other is that sex is the most awful, filthy thing on earth and you should save it for someone you love.

—*Songwriter Butch Hancock*

Science investigates; religion interprets. Science gives man knowledge, which is power; religion gives man wisdom, which is control.

—*Civil rights leader Martin Luther King Jr.*

Most people are willing to take the Sermon on the Mount as a flag to sail under, but few will use it as a rudder by which to steer.

—*Author and physician Oliver Wendell Holmes*

Results

Results are obtained by exploiting opportunities, not by solving problems.

—*Author and management theorist Peter F. Drucker*

Retaliation

I only fought with my brothers, except for once, when I fought
Bob Stirwood. He hit my brother, so I made him sit in an ant
pile. That's creative retaliation. Then his brother came, and
chased me up a tree.

—Comic actor Tim Allen, from his book
Don't Stand Too Close To A Naked Man

Revenge

What idiot said that revenge was a dish best served cold?
What matters is that you get the opportunity to serve it.
Who cares whether it's hot or cold?

—Author John Irving

The best revenge is massive success.

—*Singer and actor Frank Sinatra*

Risk

Only those who dare to fail greatly can ever achieve greatly.

—*U.S. Attorney General and New York Senator*
Robert F. Kennedy

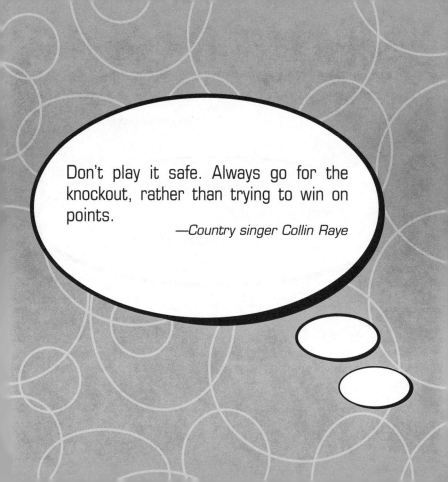

You can't play it safe forever. My daddy always told me there's only two things in the middle of the road—yellow lines and dead possums.

—*Country singer Billy Ray Cyrus*

When you face a fork in the road, step on the accelerator!

—*NBA coach Pat Riley*

Why not go out on a limb? That's where the fruit is.

—Humorist Will Rogers

Roots

It always helps to remember your roots. I remember very well how it is to pick cotton ten hours a day and to plow and cut wood. I remember it so well, I guess, because I don't intend to do it again.

—Music legend Johnny Cash

Secret of Life

The secret of life is honesty and fair dealing. If you can fake that, you've got it made.
—*Comedian Groucho Marx*

Self-Improvement

There is only one corner of the universe you can be certain of improving, and that's yourself.

—Brave New World *author Aldous Huxley*

Self-Preservation

I am not going to be a goner, so I am gone.

—*Ferdinand the Duck, from the film* Babe

Sex

There are a number of mechanical devices which increase sexual arousal, particularly in women. Chief among these is the Mercedes-Benz 380SL convertible.

—Political satirist and author P. J. O'Rourke

Sex without love is an empty experience, but as empty experiences go, it's one of the best.

—Film director Woody Allen

I think I mentioned to [a friend] I could make love for eight hours. What I didn't say was that this included four hours of begging and then dinner and a movie.

—*Music superstar Sting*

Women need a reason for having sex, men just need a place.

—*Mitch Robbins (portrayed by Billy Crystal), in the film* City Slickers

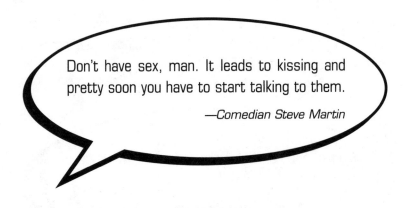

Don't have sex, man. It leads to kissing and pretty soon you have to start talking to them.

—Comedian Steve Martin

Sex is interesting, but it's not totally important. I mean, it's not even as important (physically) as excretion. A man can go seventy years without a piece of ass, but he can die in a week without a bowel movement.

—Beat writer Charles Bukowski

Men wake up aroused in the morning. We can't help it. We just wake up and we want you. And the women are thinking, "How can he want me the way I look in the morning?" It's because we can't see you. We have no blood anywhere near our optic nerve.

—*Commentator Andy Rooney*

I think men talk to women so they can sleep with them and women sleep with men so they can talk to them.

—*Author Jay McInerney*

When authorities warn you of the sinfulness of sex, there is an important lesson to be learned. Do not have sex with the authorities.

—Cartoonist and The Simpsons *creator Matt Groening*

To succeed with the opposite sex, tell her you're impotent. She can't wait to disprove it.

—Actor Cary Grant

Size

Size isn't everything. The whale is endangered, while the ant continues to do just fine.

—Kansas City Star *columnist Bill Vaughan*

It's not the size of the dog in the fight, but the size of the fight in the dog.

—5-foot-9 Ohio State star and two-time Heisman Trophy winner Archie Griffin

Skepticism

Beware the naked man who offers you his shirt.

—Business guru Harvey Mackay

Skiing

There is nothing particularly malignant in the appearance of a pair of skis. No one would guess at the possibilities which lurk in them.

—British physician, novelist, and Sherlock Holmes creator
Sir Arthur Conan Doyle

Society

What can you say about a society that says God is dead and Elvis is alive.

—Chicago Sun-Times columnist Irv Kupcinet

It is impossible to maintain civilization with 12-year-olds having babies, with 15-year-olds killing each other, with 17-year-olds dying of AIDS, and with 18-year-olds getting diplomas they can't read.

—*Former Speaker of the U.S. House of Representatives*
Newt Gingrich

Sons

You don't raise heroes, you raise sons. And if you treat them like sons, they'll turn out to be heroes, even if it's just in your own eyes.

—*Astronaut Wally Schirra's father Walter M. Schirra Sr.*

The worst waste of breath, next to playing a saxophone, is advising a son.

—*Humorist Frank McKinney "Kin" Hubbard*

Soul

If there is a soul, it is a mistake to believe that it is given to us fully created. It is created here, throughout a whole life. And living is nothing else but that long and painful bringing forth.

—*Existential French writer and 1957 Nobel Laureate in Literature Albert Camus*

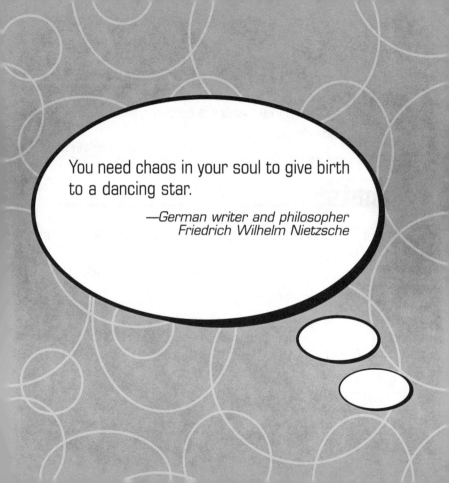

Speed of Life

It's a mere moment in a man's life between an All-Star game and an old-timer's game.

—Sportscaster Vin Scully

Sports

Serious sport has nothing to do with fair play. It is...war minus the shooting.

—British author George Orwell

I believe with all my heart that athletics is one of the finest preparations for most of the intricacies and darknesses a human life can throw at you. Athletics provide some of the richest fields of both metaphor and cliché to measure our lives against the intrusions and aggressions of other people.

—*Author Pat Conroy, from his book,* My Losing Season

stick-to-it-ness

Diamonds are nothing more than chunks of coal that stuck to their jobs.

—*Publisher and adventurer Malcolm Forbes*

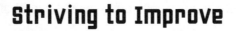

Striving to Improve

I do not try to dance better than anyone else. I only try to dance better than myself.

—Ballet dancer Mikhail Baryshnikov

struggle

Without a struggle, there can be no progress.

—Abolitionist and editor Frederick Douglass

stupidity

I don't get high, but sometimes I wish I did. That way, when I messed up in life I would have an excuse. But right now there's no rehab for stupidity.

—Actor and comedian Chris Rock

Success

What success I achieved in the theater is due to the fact that I have always worked just as hard when there were ten people in the house as when there were thousands. Just as hard in Springfield, Illinois, as on Broadway.

—African American tap dancer
Bill "Bojangles" Robinson

Summer

Summer is butter on your chin and corn mush between every tooth.

—Calvin, from the comic strip Calvin and Hobbes,
created by Bill Watterson

Survival

When you get to the end of your rope, tie a knot and hang on.

—32nd United States President Franklin Delano Roosevelt

Talent

Use the talents you possess, for the woods would be very silent if no birds sang except the best.

—Presbyterian clergyman and author Henry van Dyke

Talking

Some people without brains do an awful lot of talking.

—Scarecrow (portrayed by Ray Bolger),
in the film Wizard of Oz

Terrorism

Terrorist attacks can shake the foundations of our biggest buildings, but they cannot touch the foundation of America.

—43rd United States President George Bush, speaking to the nation after the September 11 attacks on the World Trade Center and the Pentagon

Let's suppose 10 people are killed by a small bomb on a street corner in some city in America. The first thing to understand is that there are 280 million Americans. So there's one chance in 28 (million) you're going to be one of those people. By such heartless means of calculation, the 3,000 deaths in the Twin Towers can approximate to one mortality for every 90,000 Americans. Your chances of dying if you drive a car are 1 in 7,000 each year. We seem perfectly willing to put up with auto-mobile statistics…There is a tolerable level of terror. Let's relieve ourselves of the idea that we have to remove all terror.

—Novelist Norman Mailer

Thinking

Reading furnishes the mind only with materials of knowledge; it is thinking that makes what we read ours.

—*English philosopher John Locke*

Thinking Outside the Box

I'm not afraid to think outside the box. There is a lot more space outside the box.

—*Arizona Cardinals coach Dennis Green*

Thoughtfulness

Too often we underestimate the power of a touch, a smile, a kind word, a listening ear, an honest compliment, or the smallest act of caring, all of which have the potential to turn a life around.

—*Self-help guru Leo Buscaglia*

Toughness

A lot of people are afraid to tell the truth, to say no. That's where toughness comes into play. Toughness is not being a bully. It's having backbone.

—*Millionaire Robert Kiyosaki, author of* Rich Dad Poor Dad

Trust

I never trust a man unless I've got his pecker in my pocket.

—*36th United States President Lyndon Johnson*

Truth

Truth knows no color; it appeals to intelligence.

—*African American Protestant theologian*
James Hal Cone

The men the American people admire most extravagantly are the most daring liars; the men they detest most violently are those who try to tell them the truth.

—Social critic, writer, and wit H. L. Mencken

Truth is a glorious but hard mistress. She never consults, bargains, or compromises.

—Clergyman A. W. Tozer

Twilight Zone

There is a fifth dimension beyond that which is known to man. It is a dimension as vast as space and as timeless as infinity. It is the middle ground between light and shadow, between science and superstition, and it lies at the pit of man's fear and the summit of his knowledge. This is the dimension of imagination. It is an area which we call "The Twilight Zone."

—Writer and "Twilight Zone" creator Rod Serling

Uncertainty

When in doubt, punt anyway, anywhere.

—Legendary football coach John W. Heisman, after whom the trophy for the best college football player is named

Unity

Snowflakes are frail, but if enough of them get together, they can stop traffic.

—Clergyman Dr. Vance Havner

Unknowns

Reports that say that something hasn't happened are always interesting to me, because as we know, there are known knowns; there are things we know we know. We also know there are known unknowns; that is to say we know there are some things we do not know. But there are also unknown unknowns—the ones we don't know, we don't know.

—Secretary of Defense Donald Rumsfeld
during a 2004 press conference

Violence

Violence is the first refuge of the incompetent.

—Author Isaac Asimov

Vocation

There are only three things in this world about life: find something you like to do, find something you do well, and find somebody to pay you to do it.

—College football coach Lou Holtz

Voting

We'd all like to vote for the best man but he's never a candidate.

—*Humorist Frank McKinney "Kin" Hubbard*

War

Don't be a fool and die for your country. Let the other sonofabitch die for his.

—*General George S. Patton Jr.*

What difference does it make to the dead, the orphans, and the homeless, whether the mad destruction is wrought under the name of totalitarianism or the holy name of liberty and democracy?

—*Political leader and icon of civil disobedience Mahatma Gandhi*

Older men declare war. But it's the youth who must fight and die.

—*31st United States President Herbert Hoover*

Sometimes I think war is God's way of teaching us geography.

—*Comedian Paul Rodriguez*

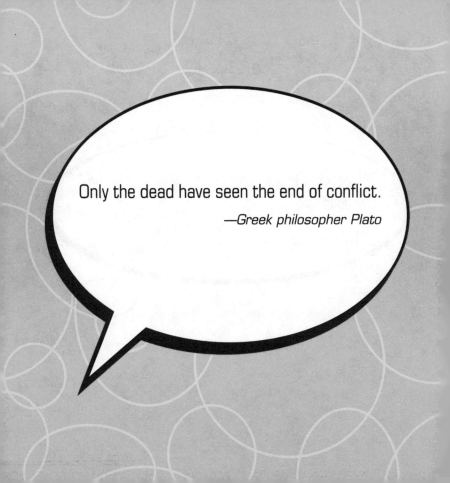

Battles are won by slaughter and maneuver. The greater the general, the more he contributes in maneuver, the less he demands in slaughter.

—British prime minister Winston Churchill

At the next war let all the Kaisers, presidents and generals and diplomats go into a big field and fight it out first among themselves. That will satisfy us and keep us at home.

—Corporal Stanislaus Katczinsky (portrayed by Louis Wolheim), in the film All Quiet on the Western Front

There are wars and then there are wars, and within every war there are wars within wars.

—*Brigadier General Ezell Ware Jr.*

Either war is obsolete or men are.

—*Architect and visionary R. Buckminster Fuller*

Waste

And Man created the plastic bag and the tin and aluminum can and the cellophane wrapper and the paper plate, and this was good because Man could then take his automobile and buy all his food in one place and He could save that which was good to eat in the refrigerator and throw away that which had no further use. And soon the earth was covered with plastic bags and aluminum cans and paper plates and disposable bottles and there was nowhere to sit down or walk, and Man shook his head and cried: "Look at this Godawful mess."

—Humorist and author Art Buchwald

Wealth

You can't have everything...where would you put it?

—Comedian Steven Wright

Whining

When I hear somebody sigh, "Life is hard," I am always tempted to ask, "Compared to what?"

—Strictly Personal *columnist Sydney J. Harris*

Wife

If you want to know about a man, you can find out an awful lot by looking at the woman he married.

—*Actor Kirk Douglas*

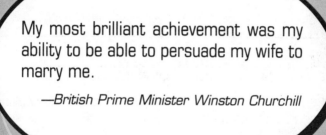

By all means marry. If you get a good wife, you'll become happy. If you get a bad one, you'll become a philosopher.

—Greek philosopher Socrates, who reportedly had a bad-tempered wife

will

Successful innovation is not a feat of intellect, but of will.

—Economist Joseph Schumpeter

You can become a winner only if you are willing to walk over the edge.

—Legendary sportswriter Damon Runyon

A winner is someone who recognizes his God-given talents, works his tail off to develop them into skills, and uses these skills to accomplish his goals.

—Boston Celtics Hall of Famer Larry Bird

Wisdom

Every man is a damn fool for at least five minutes every day; wisdom consists in not exceeding the limit.

—*Author and journalist Elbert Hubbard*

Receptionist: "How do you write women so well?"
Author Melvin Udall (portrayed by Jack Nicholson): "Easy. I think of a man, and I take away reason and accountability."

—*From the film* As Good As It Gets

Despite my thirty years of research into the feminine soul, I have not been able to answer...the great question that has never been answered: What does a woman want?

—*Founder of psychoanalysis Sigmund Freud*

Bart, a woman is like beer. They look good, they smell good, and you'd step over your own mother just to get to one.

—*TV's infamous father Homer Simpson, to his son*

Work

Nothing is really work unless you would rather be doing something else.

—*Scottish-born playwright and novelist Sir James M. Barrie,*
author of Peter Pan

A lot of fellows nowadays have a BA, MD, or PhD.
Unfortunately, they don't have a JOB.

—*Rock 'n' roll legend Fats Domino*

Never take a job where winter winds can blow
up your pants.

—*TV talk-show host and journalist*
Geraldo Rivera

World Leaders

This land is your land and this land is my land—sure, but the world is run by those that never listen to music anyway.

—Songwriter and performer Bob Dylan

Worry

Y'all don't worry, 'cause it ain't gonna be all right nohow.

—Country western legend Hank Williams

Writing

I write when I'm inspired, and I see to it that I'm inspired at 9 o'clock every morning.

—*Short-story writer and novelist Peter de Vries*

Xenophobia

Remember that when you say, "I will have none of this exile and this stranger for his face is not like my face and his speech is strange," you have denied America with that word.

—*Poet and author Stephen Vincent Benét*

Yelling

Yelling at living things does tend to kill the spirit in them. Sticks and stones may break our bones, but words will break our hearts.

—*Theologian, philosopher, and author Robert Fulghum, from his book* All I Really Need to Know I Learned in Kindergarten

Zeal is a volcano, on the peak of which the grass of indecisiveness does not grow.

—*Lebanese-born writer Kahlil Gibran, author of* The Prophet

Allan Zullo is the bestselling author of over 80 books, including *The Sports Hall of Shame* series, which has sold over 2 million copies, and *The Boomers' Guide to Grandparenting*. He has been creating and producing bestselling daily calendars since 1989. He has appeared on hundreds of radio and television shows including *Good Morning America*, *The Today Show* and *David Letterman*. He lives in Fairview, NC.